MUNICH

Dan Colwell

JPMGUIDES

Contents

- **This Way Munich** — 3
- **Flashback** — 7
- **Sightseeing** — 13
- **Altstadt** — 14
- **Residenz** — 23
- **Königsplatz** — 28
- **Schwabing** — 33
- **Englischer Garten** — 36
- **Haidhausen** — 39
- **Around Munich** — 41
- **Excursions** — 46
- **Dining Out** — 50
- **Entertainment** — 58
- **The Hard Facts** — 64
- **Index** — 71–72

Fold-out map
Munich,
Old Town,
Upper Bavaria

This Way Munich

The Bavarian Good Life
From the moment you arrive you'll notice that there's something different about Munich. It has a sunny, easy-going, southern vivacity not typically associated with its more serious counterparts elsewhere in Germany. Indeed, it's often referred to as Italy's northernmost city, and that is not simply because of the large number of Italian tourists and workers who flock here from just across the Alps. Munich expresses perfectly what the Germans call *Gemütlichkeit* —that comfortable, warm embrace you'll feel as soon as you walk into Marienplatz, the old town square, or sit outside a café in the Bohemian quarter of Schwabing, or pop into one of the fine beer halls or beer gardens around town. You will suddenly become aware that the citizens of this beautiful city have discovered the knack of enjoying the Good Life, in all its earthy Bavarian richness.

The ambience is enhanced by a healthy dose of German-influenced culture. What you'll be drinking and eating at those bars and cafés is not so much wine and pasta as the delicious Bavarian specialities, *Weissbier* and *Weisswurst*, while all round you—from the efficient public transport system to the gleaming shopping centres—you'll find evidence of the fearsomely successful industrial society that Munich undoubtedly is.

How the city has managed to achieve the best of both worlds is readily explained. Bavaria, as any local will happily tell you, is not simply part of Germany, but rather its own place with its own cultural identity. Until 1918, there was a Bavarian monarchy and government separate from the rest of the nation, and the region maintains a proud tradition of independence to this day. Its ability to combine triumphantly the finer aspects of north and south is testament to the Bavarian national character. Munich's ability to play as hard as it works is, for the visitor, nothing less than an invitation to sample the Good Life in the company of those who have perfected the art.

City of Paradoxes
Before long, you'll realize that Munich is something of a riddle. As the Bavarian capital, it's the political and social core of a predominantly Catholic region with a largely rural and conservative population. But it also lies at the principal cultural crossroads of

Europe, and is one of the most open and cosmopolitan cities of the continent.

For almost eight centuries it was the personal domain of the autocratic Wittelsbach dynasty. What began as a small Bavarian market town became the terrain on which their aspirations to imperial status could be visibly marked out. Huge palaces, baroque churches, wide boulevards and imposing neoclassical monuments and museums were built over the years. Munich also acquired some of Europe's finest collections of art and antiquities. Furthermore, from the beginning of the 20th century it attracted many of Germany's best artists and writers and, along with them, the liberal, worldly atmosphere that it has retained ever since. After World War II, with Berlin divided, it was Germany's unofficial capital, the liveliest spot in the country and with a booming high-tech economy to match—BMW and Siemens are based here, as are Germany's film, media, publishing and fashion industries.

And yet alongside this dynamic modern metropolis, a different Munich continues to thrive—the old market town that never really changed. You can see it still in the number of people who favour traditional *Lederhosen* over Munich's haute couture, who sing along with oompah bands in old beer halls rather than sip cocktails in trendy Schwabing bars. Its supreme expression is the world-famous Oktoberfest, during which Bavarian thigh-slapping, beer-glass-clinking revelries provide as powerful an image of the city as sleek BMW cars or its great art galleries.

The real attraction, however, lies in exploring both sides of Munich's character—by far the most entertaining way to solve the puzzle of this intriguing city.

Festival City

One of the great things about Munich is the astonishing variety of things going on. There are so many festivals throughout the year it seems almost as if it's involved in one continuous jamboree. The biggest of them all is the Oktoberfest, when for 16 days more than 6.1 million litres of beer will be consumed by 6 million visitors from around the globe—the entire proceedings enlivened by processions, Bavarian brass bands and funfairs. Just as exuberant, *Fasching* is the city's rollicking pre-Lenten carnival, which begins on January 7 and lasts for six weeks. There are parades, fancy-dress balls and stage shows, culminating in a huge city-wide party on Shrove Tuesday.

These earthy Bavarian festivals are counterbalanced by

This Way Munich

Ten times Prost! The October beer festival is not for the faint-hearted.

Munich's heavyweight cultural events. The city is a leading centre for opera, ballet and music, with three internationally renowned orchestras and the prestigious Opera Festival that takes place in July. Year-round, the numerous art galleries and museums put on world-class exhibitions of art, from Ancient Greek to the avant-garde.

If jazz is more your style, you can hear it played in major theatres in the centre of town or smoky little bars in Schwabing and Haidhausen. Or perhaps you prefer the cinema? The Munich Film Festival is one of the most respected in Europe. Nightclubs? The remarkable Kultfabrik complex, grouping twenty-odd discotheques and clubs on one site matches anything New York, London or Berlin can offer.

And if all this isn't enough to keep you happy, you can always head south to the lakes and the Alps less than an hour away, where hiking, windsurfing and sailing in summer and skiing in winter should satisfy the most avid sports-enthusiast, while dreamers can explore Ludwig II's fairytale castles.

Perhaps, the hardest thing for visitors to Munich is that there is just too much to choose from.

Flashback

Early History
Munich traces its origins to a small, 8th-century settlement established by monks from the Benedictine monastery at Lake Tegern—its name derives from *ze den Munichen*, meaning simply "home of the monks". It remained a backwater until the 1150s, when Henry the Lion, Duke of Bavaria, chose it as the place from which to mount a bid to control the profitable salt trade from Salzburg. Until then, salt tolls had been collected by the bishop of Freising at the bridge at Föhring. Henry destroyed the bridge and built his own over the River Isar at Munich, at the same time granting the monks the right to establish a marketplace and mint money. Henry's cousin, the German Emperor Frederick Barbarossa, officially sanctioned the duke's bold move on June 14, 1158, a date now looked on as the city's foundation—though the unhappy bishop had to be appeased with a third of the tolls.

The Rise of the Wittelsbachs
Munich boomed on the back of the salt trade, but arrogance finally brought down its founder. Henry refused to aid Barbarossa's foreign campaigns and was consequently dispossessed of his city in 1180. Munich was handed over to a staunch servant of the emperor, Count Otto von Wittelsbach, whose family were to rule Bavaria until 1918.

The Wittelsbachs made Munich their capital in 1255 under Duke Ludwig II the Stern, and it increasingly took on the trappings of a major city, with a large ducal residence, part of which survives today as the Alter Hof. Things developed further under Duke Ludwig IV the Bavarian, who became Holy Roman Emperor in 1328. Munich was now home to an imperial court and attracted scholars and merchants from around Europe. Ludwig also expanded the city, building a second ring of walls that marked the city limits for the next 450 years.

Tumult in the Middle Ages
Bavarian territory was whittled away after Ludwig the Bavarian's death by its division among family members, a situation not remedied until the law of primogeniture (whereby the firstborn inherits the property) was instituted in 1506. These partitions lost Bavaria power and prestige in the region, although the biggest threat to the city came from the plague.

The Black Death arrived in 1348 to devastating effect, creating economic and political turmoil that would last for more than a century. Irrational acts of revenge for the plague were taken out on Jews, leading to pogroms and mass emigration. An uprising against the Wittelsbachs was begun in 1397 by the artisans and small tradesmen, leading to the temporary exile of the city's patricians. It was eventually put down by military force, and it was in the face of such dangers from their own subjects that the Wittelsbachs had the huge fortress of the Residenz palace constructed.

Counter-Reformation and Renaissance

Life slowly returned to normal in the 15th century. A renewed prosperity under Duke Albrecht IV the Wise saw the construction of many of Munich's finest buildings, including the great Frauenkirche and the Altes Rathaus, completed in the 1470s. Albrecht's successor, Duke Wilhelm IV (ruled 1508–50), was a fierce defender of the Catholic faith and brought all his power to bear upon resisting the Reformation which, inspired by the revolutionary teachings of Martin Luther, was in full flow in northern Germany. Protestant heretics were sought out, arrested and executed, and Munich became the centre of Germany's Counter-Reformation.

In tandem with this political and social conservatism came the onset of the Bavarian Renaissance. Wilhelm and the next two dukes, Albrecht V and Wilhelm V, were patrons of the arts which, they believed, were a powerful means of underpinning the Counter-Reformation. They established the Bavarian State Library and Jesuit School, and built the mighty Renaissance-style Michaelskirche, although in so doing nearly emptied the national coffers.

War and Plague

It was left to Maximilian I to pay off the Wittelsbachs' debts. He did so within 12 years of becoming duke in 1597, and also managed to acquire the superb art collection that became the basis of the Alte Pinakothek, richly embellish the Residenz and still find time to lead the Catholic League in the Thirty Years' War. His successes in battle earned him the title of Prince Elector in 1623, but matters took a turn for the worse nine years later when the Swedes under Gustavus Adolphus invaded Munich. After they left, the city was in chaos, facing starvation and having to pay a huge sum of money to Adolphus. Weakened by war, Müncheners easily succumbed to the plague of 1634, which killed off one-third of the population. When the plague finally loosened its grip a few years later, Maximilian had the Mariensäule column erected in the Marienplatz as a symbol of thanksgiving.

The late 17th and 18th centuries saw Bavarian finances reaching new lows, as the Prince Electors took the state into more wars. Bavaria assisted the Habsburg Austrians in relieving the Turkish siege of Vienna in 1683, and then entered the War of Spanish Succession (1701–14) in support of the French against Austria. Unfortunately, it was the losing side, and Bavaria suffered the indignity of being occupied for 10 years by the Austrians. When Bavarian peasants rebelled, the Habsburg armies carried out a bloody massacre, and the leaders were publicly executed on Marienplatz.

Though there was considerable hardship among the peasants and workers throughout the period, it was also a time when Munich flowered as a city of the baroque, with extravagant architectural gestures in both church and aristocratic buildings. In the face of such splendid baroque confections as the Theatinerkirche, Schloss Nymphenburg, the Asam church and the remarkable rococo Cuvilliéstheater, the patricians could, perhaps, ignore the grimmer social realities of contemporary Munich life.

Royal Capital

The first rumblings of change came from an unlikely source. Though the shock waves of the French Revolution had hardly caused a ripple in Bavaria, Maximilian IV Joseph (ruled 1799–1825) had a rude awakening in 1800 when Napoleon's troops arrived at the gates of the city. The duke fled, returning only after deciding to ally himself with the French. Napoleon himself visited to great acclaim in 1805 en route to the Battle of Austerlitz, after which he elevated his Bavarian ally to the status of kingdom, and Maximilian was crowned the first King of Bavaria.

The kingdom made considerable territorial gains through this link with Napoleon, which it kept thanks to a timely switch of allegiance to the Germanic Confederation in 1813 just prior to his defeat. Nonetheless, elements of France's more egalitarian spirit had entered Bavarian political life, leading to a new constitution and a Bill of Rights in 1818 that introduced limited parliamentary democracy and guaranteed religious equality for Protestants.

The city was in fact just entering its heyday. It was transformed by Maximilian's son, Ludwig I (reigned 1825–48), into a neoclassical royal capital, with wide boulevards, large squares, world-renowned museums and the foundation of Munich University. Ludwig also fostered the development of the industrial revolution in Bavaria, with the first railway in Germany opening between Munich and Augsburg in 1840. His delight in modernity didn't extend to politics, however, and his increasingly absolutist manner alienated many sections of Munich society. The younger, radical set were enthused with the liberal ideas sweeping Europe in 1848, the so-called Year of Revolution; but the conservatives were equally dismayed by Ludwig's behaviour, when his love affair with an Irish dancer known as Lola Montez, a woman half his age, became public. It was this, not revolution, that led to his abdication.

Art and War

Under Ludwig's successors, Munich became one of Europe's most prominent artistic cities. His grandson, Ludwig II, is now famous as the builder of fantasy castles around Bavaria, but his dreams were fuelled by a love of music and the desire to make Munich into a shrine to his idol, Richard Wagner. Several of Wagner's operas received their world premieres in the city, but Ludwig's plan to finance a special theatre for the performance of Wagner's music was vetoed by the city authorities and the king was forced to send the great composer into exile.

Ludwig's political judgements went equally awry. His decision to side with Austria in the Austro-Prussian war of 1866 gave the victorious Prussians and their indefatigable Chancellor, Otto von Bismarck, enormous leverage in Bavaria. When war against France began four years later, Bavaria had little choice but to follow Prussia's lead, and in 1871 it was incorporated into the new German Empire under Kaiser Wilhelm I. Ludwig kept his title, though not for long. His castle-building spree was draining the Bavarian treasury, and in 1886 the government intervened and had him declared insane. The king was taken to Schloss Berg, where soon afterwards he and his doctor drowned in Lake Starnberg. Whether he was murdered or committed suicide has never been determined.

Ludwig's brother, Otto, was already certified as insane, and so his uncle Luitpold took over as regent. During this period the Munich art world reached new heights. The *Blaue Reiter* group emerged, including artists such as Wassily Kandinsky, Paul Klee and Franz Marc, while the bohemian Schwabing district was home to the writers Thomas Mann, Franz Wedekind and Rainer Maria Rilke. The cultural effervescence of the city was matched in the political arena, and just before the outbreak of World War I, Lenin was here editing an underground newspaper, while the revolutionary Rosa Luxembourg voiced the complaints of Munich's poor and unemployed. Attracted by all this excitement, a would-be artist called Adolf Hitler came to Munich fresh from artistic failure in Vienna.

Unsurprisingly, the onset of World War I set off this cultural powder keg. Munich was convulsed by political upheavals from which it would take many decades to recover.

Munich and the Third Reich

When Luitpold died in 1912, his son became King Ludwig III. Following the social chaos that came with defeat at the end of the war, 100,000 workers and peasants met on Theresienwiese in November 1918 and marched on the Residenz. Led by the socialist leader Kurt Eisner, they stormed the palace and the last reigning Wittelsbach fled Bavaria and abdicated five days later. A People's Republic was declared, with Eisner as its prime minister, but violent infighting among the many political factions meant the new government soon disintegrated, and after just three months Eisner was assassinated. A Soviet-style republic (the *Räterepublik*) was declared and lasted till May 1919. In its wake came the brutal White Guard counter-revolution carried out by German army units and the volunteer *Freikorps*.

Matters seemed to be resolved in August 1919, when a new constitution saw Bavaria join the Weimar Republic. But Munich's volatile political life continued, with many violently nationalist parties ready to cause trouble when the right moment offered itself. One of them, the Deutsche Arbeiter-Partei (DAP) met at the famous Hofbräuhaus in central Munich. It was as a member of the DAP, soon to be renamed the Nazi Party, that Hitler first rose to prominence. In November 1923, backed by 600 stormtroopers, he attempted to seize power in Bavaria in the Beer Hall Putsch. The uprising started at the Bürgerbräukeller on Rosenheimerstrasse with the kidnapping of the Bavarian Minister-President, but it came to an inglorious end the next day at the Feldherrnhalle, when the Bavarian police easily crushed Hitler's troops.

Hitler was arrested and sentenced to five years in nearby Landsberg prison. That might well have been the end of his career as a demagogue, except that Bavaria was notoriously right-wing and Hitler found himself something of a hero to be accorded special treatment. He was given the freedom to write *Mein Kampf* and served just one year of his term. Hitler later moved to Berlin, but Munich remained the Nazis' headquarters. In the 1930s, after he became German Chancellor, it was made the *Haupstadt der Bewegung*—Capital of the [Nazi] Movement. The city had the dubious honour of being home to the first Nazi concentration camp, which opened at Dachau in March 1933. And it was in the Nazi headquarters on Arcisstrasse that the British and French leaders, Neville Chamberlain and Edouard Daladier, signed the infamous 1938 Munich Agreement with Hitler, agreeing to the dismemberment of Czechoslovakia.

During the war, political activity was mainly focused on Berlin, but there were a few noble pockets of resistance to the Nazis in Munich, not least the condemnatory pronouncements from the pulpit of the Michaelskirche by Father Rupert Mayer. From 1942, the city was relentlessly bombed by the Allies, and most of its ancient buildings were destroyed. At the end of the war, the American army occupied the demoralized city, and it became part of the new Federal Republic of West Germany in 1948.

Rising from the Ashes

The reconstruction of Munich—architectural, economic and psychological—has been little short of miraculous. A decision was made early on to rebuild the city in its old form rather than start anew, and such marvels as the Frauenkirche and the Altes Rathaus were painstakingly pieced together from the rubble.

During the Cold War Munich became West Germany's most cosmopolitan city, a sort of surrogate capital. This was underpinned by its powerhouse economy, based on high-tech giants such as BMW, MAN, Bayer and Siemens. Its post-war coming of age occurred in 1972, when it played host to the Olympic Games and appeared before the world as a gleamingly efficient modern city. But throughout this time it has managed to retain its essential Bavarian identity. Certainly, Munich is a city that is able to look forward confidently to a successful future, while never losing sight of the traditions of its historic Bavarian past.

Sightseeing

The Altstadt (Old Town) occupies the site of medieval Munich. Beyond here the later municipal developments fan out in an arc. They can all be easily reached by Munich's excellent public transport network.

14 **Altstadt**: the geographical heart of the modern metropolis

23 **Residenz**: stronghold of the Wittelsbach dynasty

28 **Königsplatz**: monumental art galleries and museums

33 **Schwabing**: once Bohemian and still resolutely trendy

36 **Englischer Garten**: a vast city park that's a study in elegance

39 **Haidhausen**: across the Isar, the old working-class district, home to the huge Gasteig arts complex and the liveliest nightspot in town

41 **Around Munich**: parks and palaces, film studios and Oktoberfest

ALTSTADT

The Altstadt was once enclosed by city walls put up in the reign of Duke Ludwig the Bavarian, and three of the original medieval gates—Karlstor, Sendlinger Tor and Isartor—remain to this day at its western, southern and eastern edges. The northern limit is marked by Odeonsplatz, laid out in the 19th century as part of Ludwig I's building spree. To walk from any one of these points to another takes no more than 20 minutes. But with a host of fascinating things to see whichever direction you follow, the journey is sure to last enjoyably longer. The sights below are described in a clockwise direction starting at Marienplatz, the natural place to begin any tour.

Marienplatz D–E 5*
U-Bahn, S-Bahn Marienplatz

With its vast town hall as a backdrop, and buskers, street entertainers and a famous performing Glockenspiel at centre stage, Marienplatz is pure theatre. This is where many of the city's most dramatic moments have been played out ever since Duke Henry the Lion first granted Benedictine monks the right to hold a market back in 1158. Formerly called the Schrannenplatz (Corn Exchange), it was for centuries the site of the city's grain market, as well as the scene of public executions, jousting competitions and the *Schäfflertanz* (cooper's dance). The first dance occurred in 1517 to celebrate the end of the plague, and has been performed every seven years ever since—the next one is in 2012.

In the middle of the square, the **Mariensäule** (Column of the Virgin Mary) was put up by Maximilian I in 1638. It's a thanksgiving to Bavaria's patron saint for sparing Munich from the ravages of invading Swedish troops during the Thirty Years' War and the plague that followed. The shining figure of Mary on top dates from 1594 and originally made up part of the Frauenkirche's high altar. At the base are four baroque *putti*, muscular cherubs who symbolically battle with plague, war, hunger and heresy as represented by a basilisk, lion, dragon and serpent.

A longstanding meeting-place as well as a good spot to sit and cool off is the **Fischbrunnen** (Fish Fountain) in the northeast corner of the square. Until the end of the

---
*References correspond to the fold-out map at the end of the guide.

Altstadt

19th century, it was where new butchers' apprentices had to undergo an initiation ceremony by leaping into the water.

Neues Rathaus D 5
- U-Bahn, S-Bahn Marienplatz
- Tower open May–Oct Mon–Fri 9 a.m.– 7 p.m., Sat, Sun 10 a.m.– 7 p.m.; rest of year Mon–Thurs 9 a.m.–4 p.m., Fri 9 a.m.–1 p.m. Glockenspiel daily at 11 a.m., noon, 5 p.m.; in winter at 11 a.m. and noon

The New Town Hall, built between 1867 and 1908, dominates Marienplatz. Its neo-Gothic façade is populated with statues of Bavarian kings, local dignitaries and legendary characters. Halfway up the 85-m (279-ft) tower is one of Munich's biggest tourist draws, a two-tier Glockenspiel with 32 mechanical figures. The top part re-enacts the marriage of Duke Wilhelm V and Renata of Lorraine, which took place here in 1568 along with lavish festivities that included a knights' tournament. Below this, the cooper's perform their famous dance. If you turn up at 9 p.m. you'll witness a nightwatchman, with horn and lantern, and the Angel of Peace signal bedtime for the *Münchner Kindl*, the little monk who is the city mascot.

The main entrance leads to an attractive neo-Gothic courtyard, with a tranquil open-air café. Just inside the entrance, an elevator takes you in two stages to the tower's ninth floor, where there are stunning views across the city's rooftops and spires all the way to the Alps when the föhn blows.

Altes Rathaus D 5
- U-Bahn, S-Bahn Marienplatz
- Toy Museum open daily 10 a.m.–5.30 p.m. (closed Christmas Eve and Mardi Gras)

The Old Town Hall, on the square's eastern side, was built in 1470–80 by Jörg von Halsbach and is famed for its Gothic main hall, where the city's elite held dances. The building was destroyed during World War II, and the organ-pipe gables and green pinnacles are reconstructions from the 1950s. The tower, which also serves as a gateway, was completed in 1975 and modelled on the Gothic original. It now houses the **Spielzeugmuseum** (Toy Museum) displaying dolls, teddy bears, puppets and other toys.

Alter Hof E 5
- U-Bahn, S-Bahn Marienplatz

From the Altes Rathaus, ancient Burgstrasse leads to the Alter Hof. En route, be sure to take a look at No. 5 Burgstrasse, a rare late-Gothic house dating from 1550 and now a tavern. The building next door at No. 7 was the residence of Mozart while he was composing *Idomeneo*, which had its premiere in Munich in 1781.

Entrance to the Alter Hof is through the Burgtor (City Gate), leading into an attractive medieval courtyard, later integrated into the Wittelsbachs' first town residence. It is uncannily calm for such a central location. If the towers have a rather Disneyesque look about them, it's because they underwent a less than sensitive neo-Gothic renovation in the 19th century.

Hofbräuhaus E 5
- U-Bahn, S-Bahn Marienplatz
- Platzl 9
- Open daily 9 a.m.–11.30 p.m.

Continue eastwards from the Alter Hof to the ever-popular Platzl, a small square packed with taverns and restaurants. The Hofbräuhaus makes a justifiable claim to be Munich's most famous beer hall. It has been serving up huge mugs of Bavarian beer in this building since the 1890s and is frequented by locals and tourists alike.

There are large upper floors where you can hear live Bavarian oompah music in the summer, plus a shady inner beer garden.

It's all good clean fun now, but during the early 1920s this was a major venue for political meetings held by Munich's extremist parties, and the scene of many a vicious brawl. The Festsaal on the top floor was where, on February 24, 1920, the then unknown Adolf Hitler gave his first major speech to a large public meeting, the success of which set him off on the path to power.

Valentin-Karlstadt-Musäum E 5
- S-Bahn Isartor
- Tram 17 Isartor
- 1st floor of the tower
- Mon, Tues 11.01 a.m.–5.29 p.m.;
- Fri, Sat 11.01 a.m.–19.59 p.m.;
- Sun 10.01 a.m.–5.29 p.m.
- First Fri in month to 9.59 p.m.
- Tel. 22 32 66

Head south to Im Tal and make for the south tower of the medieval Isartor, where this museum's eccentric opening times give a good indication of its nature. Karl Valentin (1882–1948) was a type of German Charlie Chaplin of the 1920s, an irreverent, slapstick comedian loved by Munich's workers and intellectuals alike—Bertold Brecht and Herman Hesse were both devoted fans. Liesl Karlstadt (1892–1960) was his partner. The museum can be hard work for non-German speakers, although its junk-shop appearance,

Altstadt

Taking a break from shopping in the Viktualienmarkt.

crammed with old stage props, and pictures of Valentin's undoubtedly comic face, give a flavour of the comedian's wacky style. What's more, you can finish with coffee and cakes or a white sausage at one of the city's most enjoyable cafés, the Valentinsmusäumsstubl (tel. 29 37 62), at the top of the tower.

Bier- und Oktoberfestmuseum E 5
- U-Bahn Marienplatz
- S-Bahn Isartor
- Tram 17 Isartor
- Sterneckerstrasse 2
- Wed–Sun 11 a.m.–5 p.m.
- Tel. 24 23 16 07

In one of Munich's oldest patrician houses, an exhibition that will tell you more than you ever wanted to know about beer and its history. In the café you can sample beer and snacks (Tues–Sat 5 p.m.–midnight).

Heiliggeistkirche E 5
- U-Bahn, S-Bahn Marienplatz
- Tal 77
- Mon–Fri 6.30–7 p.m.;
- Sat, Sun 8 a.m.–7 p.m.

The Church of the Holy Spirit (1392) is a large Gothic hall church which succumbed to Munich's insatiable appetite for the baroque in the 18th century. The renovation was striking, with a remarkable painted ceiling by Egid Quirin Asam and his brother Cosmas Damian and a sumptuous rococo high altar of 1730. The most valued treasure, however, is the Marienalter in the north aisle, with its *Hammerthaler Muttergottes,* a wooden sculpture of the Virgin Mary carved in 1450 and brought here from Lake Tegern monastery.

Viktualienmarkt E 5
- U-Bahn, S-Bahn Marienplatz
- Bus 52 Viktualienmarkt

This huge, exuberant food market—one of the largest in Europe—has occupied the former courtyard of the Heiliggeistkirche since the beginning of the 19th century. The colourful stalls sell cheese, fruit and vegetables, delicatessen, meat and spices of outstanding quality and at prices to match, though you'll probably get an earful of Bavarian dialect thrown in at no extra cost. The market also contains a beer garden and good places to buy snacks. Look out for statues of Munich's past folk entertainers, such as the comedian Karl Valentin and his sidekick Liesl Karlstadt.

Peterskirche D–E 5
- U-Bahn, S-Bahn Marienplatz
- Rindermarkt 1
- Daily (except Wed afternoon) 7 a.m.–7 p.m.
- Tower Mon–Sat 9 a.m.–7 p.m.; Sun 10 a.m.–6 p.m.; holidays 10 a.m.–7 p.m. (in winter to 6 p.m.)

Munich's oldest church is known affectionately as Alter Peter (Old Peter) and dates from 1368. It was built on the site of an 11th-century church in contemporary Gothic style, although the highly distinctive 92-m (300-ft) rectangular tower is a later addition of 1607. The views from the top surpass even those from the Rathaus, though you'll have to climb each of its 300 steps on foot. The church's interior was given a rococo revamp in the 18th century, with a dazzling high altar by one of Munich's leading sculptors at the time, Egid Quirin Asam. The altar incorporates a figure of St Peter carved in 1492 by Erasmus Grasser, as well as Asam's statues of the four Church Fathers. The original high altar once included five late-Gothic panels by Jan Polack showing scenes from the life of St Peter; they now adorn the presbytery walls.

Münchner Stadtmuseum D 5
- U-Bahn, S-Bahn Marienplatz
- Bus 57 Marienplatz
- St.-Jakobs-Platz 1
- Tues–Sun 10 a.m.–6 p.m.
- Tel. 23 32 23 70

Altstadt

Located in the 15th-century city arsenal, the Municipal Museum provides fascinating insight into Munich's lively history. The highlight is without doubt the Morisken-Saal next to the entrance hall, with 10 Gothic statues of Morris dancers carved by Erasmus Grasser in 1480. They once looked down on Munich's patricians at the stately dances held in the main hall of the Altes Rathaus, and their contorted figures have since become familiar figures in the city, with countless replicas made.

There's also an extensive collection of puppets on the third floor, in addition to rooms dedicated to photography and film, musical instruments and fashion.

Asamkirche D 5
- U-Bahn Sendlinger Tor
- Sendlinger Strasse 32
- Daily 7.30 a.m.–7 p.m.

Just before the medieval Sendlinger Tor gateway is a church built by the Asam brothers as their private chapel. Here they created one of the finest and most coherent expressions of South German rococo architecture. Completed in 1746, it was dedicated to St John Nepomuk, whose statue is over the entrance. The narrow interior stuns the senses, its every inch covered with frescoes, sculptures, gilt and stucco, the eye thoroughly tricked into seeing something far grander than the actual dimensions allow. The house of Egid Quirin Asam is next door and has a splendid rococo façade designed by him.

Jüdisches Museum München E 6
- U-Bahn Sendlinger Tor
- S-Bahn Marienplatz
- St.-Jakobs-Platz 1
- Tel. 23 32 81 89
- Due to open in March 2007
- www.juedisches-museum.muenchen.de

Permanent exhibition documenting the history of Munich Jews, and smaller temporary exhibitions, moved from its former home on Reichenbachstrasse to a new complex, which will include a Jewish community centre, a synagogue, library, bookshop and café.

Kaufingerstrasse and Neuhauser Strasse D 5
- U-Bahn, S-Bahn Marienplatz or Karlsplatz

Leading west off Marienplatz, Munich's main shopping precinct was laid out as a pedestrian zone in 1972. It's a bustling stretch of department stores, clothes and shoe shops, boutiques and restaurants running all the way to Karlstor at the boundary of the Altstadt.

Sightseeing

Frauenkirche (Dom) D 5

- U-Bahn, S-Bahn Marienplatz
- Frauenplatz
- Open daily 7 a.m.–9 p.m.;
- Thurs to 8.30 p.m.; Fri to 6 p.m.;
- lift in south tower (closed Sun and holidays) Apr–Oct. Mon–Sat
- 10 a.m.–5 p.m.

The onion-domed twin towers of Munich's mighty red-brick cathedral are the most instantly recognizable feature of the city skyline. They were completed in 1488, 20 years after the Frauenkirche's first stone was laid, though the domes weren't added until 1525. At 99 m (325 ft) they are the tallest edifices in the Altstadt—a by-law prohibits any other building going higher. Take the lift up the south tower for yet another panoramic view of the city, and a close-up of the north tower. Inside the entrance, look out for the Devil's Footprint. Legend has it that the architect, Jörg von Halsbach, tricked the Devil into giving him the money to complete the church, the mark in the paving-stone being the result of the Devil stamping his foot in rage when he found out. Oddly enough, it looks as if he must have been wearing a size 10 boot at the time, although there is a tell-tale claw-mark visible.

Nearby, the tomb of Ludwig IV the Bavarian is one of the most striking monuments in an otherwise fairly austere interior. It was made out of bronze and black marble in 1622, nearly three centuries after Ludwig's death, under the auspices of the ambitious Maximilian I—a clever piece of propaganda during the Thirty Years' War to remind people that a Wittelsbach had once been Holy Roman Emperor.

The Frauenkirche was badly damaged during World War II, but the superb Gothic stained-glass windows in the choir had already been taken out for safe keeping. Other notable survivors from the early days are Erasmus Grasser's characteristically powerful wooden sculptures in the choir stalls (1502), an automatic clock dating from about 1500, possibly by Grasser as well, and altar panels by Jan Polack.

Deutsches Jagd- und Fischereimuseum D 5

- U-Bahn, S-Bahn Marienplatz
- Neuhauser Strasse 2
- Open daily 9.30 a.m.–5 p.m.;
- Thurs 9.30 a.m.–9 p.m.
- Tel. 22 05 22

Follow Frauenplatz round to where Kaufingerstrasse meets Neuhauser Strasse, and you'll spot the large bronze boar outside the museum entrance. Located in a 13th-century Augustinian abbey with rococo embellishments, the museum is dedicated to hunting and fishing.

Michaelskirche D 5
- U-Bahn, S-Bahn Marienplatz or Karlsplatz
- Neuhauser Strasse 52
- Daily 8.30 a.m.–7 p.m;
- Sun to 10 p.m.

St Michael's Church was built by Jesuits under the patronage of Duke Wilhelm V between 1583 and 1597, and the cost nearly bankrupted the state. What the Bavarians got for their money was a perfect monument to the Counter-Reformation's triumph over north German Lutheranism. The superb Renaissance façade has a sculpture by Hubert Gerhard above the main doors showing the Archangel Michael defeating Satan (symbolic of the Catholic Church crushing Martin Luther), while other niches in the gable honour Wilhelm, who holds a model of the church in his hand, and his Wittelsbach ancestors. Inside, the pillarless barrel-vaulted nave gives the church an enormous sense of light and space. In its day, it was on a scale second only to St Peter's in Rome.
The side chapels have a series of 16th-century paintings, while the pulpit and altar are unashamedly baroque. The left transept is dominated by the huge, neoclassical monument to Eugène de Beauharnais, the stepson of Napoleon, while the crypt contains the Wittelsbach tombs, including those of Wilhelm V and Mad King Ludwig II, permanently honoured with flowers and a lit candle.
Next to the church, the **Alte Akademie** (Old Academy) was once the Jesuit school, founded by Wilhelm V after he had invited the Jesuits to Munich in 1559 to spearhead the Counter-Reformation. The Richard Strauss Fountain (1962) in front of the Academy commemorates Munich's greatest composer, and features scenes from his opera *Salomé*.

Bürgersaal D 5
- U-Bahn, S-Bahn Karlsplatz
- Neuhauser Strasse 48
- Open daily;
- Upper chapel 9 a.m.– 4 p.m.
- Lower chapel 8.30 a.m.–7 p.m.

This early 18th-century meeting hall further along Neuhauser Strasse was used by theology students of the Marian brotherhood.
The upper chapel is decorated in grand baroque style, with fine guardian angels on both the stairways leading up to it, sculpted by Ignaz Günther in 1763.
The simple lower chapel is the object of greater veneration, as it contains the tomb of Rupert Mayer, the priest persecuted for his resolutely anti-Nazi sermons given in the 1930s and 1940s.

Sightseeing

Around Karlsplatz D 4
- U-Bahn, S-Bahn Karlsplatz
- Tram 19 Karlsplatz

Pass through Karlstor to the open expanse of Karlsplatz, laid out in 1791 and named after the Elector Karl Theodor. His general unpopularity can be inferred from the fact that the locals preferred to call it "Stachus", after Eustachius Föderl who kept an inn on this site—a name that is still widely used. The square contains some fine neo-baroque architecture, in particular the massive **Justizpalast** (Palace of Justice) building (1891–97) on the north side. Take the escalator beneath the square to find a vast subterranean **shopping centre**.
Behind the Palace of Justice, the **Alter Botanischer Garten** was once the treasured green space of the city's western suburbs, until a larger and less traffic-burdened botanical garden was built further out in 1909. It still makes for a pleasant shady break from the hubbub, graced with the attractive Neptune Fountain and an outdoor café.
A short distance from the entrance gateway, on Lenbachplatz, the **Wittelsbacher Brunnen** is a magnificent neoclassical fountain completed in 1895 by Adolf von Hildebrand.

Dreifaltigkeitskirche D 4
- U-Bahn, S-Bahn Karlsplatz
- Tram 19 Lenbachplatz
- Pacellistrasse 12
- Open daily 7 a.m.–7 p.m.

The exquisite Italianate baroque Trinity Church was built between 1711 and 1718 to a design by Giovanni Antonio Viscardi. The brilliant interior has a fine dome fresco by Cosmas Damian Asam.

Around Promenadeplatz D 4
- U-Bahn, S-Bahn Karlsplatz
- Tram 19 Lenbachplatz

The best-known building on this elegant square, the neoclassical **Palais Montgelas** (1810–11), is now incorporated into the upmarket Bayerischer Hof Hotel. Nearby, the **Palais Portia** dates from the 1690s and was later given as a lavish present by the Elector Karl Albrecht to his mistress, Princess Portia. It had a rococo facelift in 1737 courtesy of the great Belgian-born, Munich-based architect François de Cuvilliés.
A short walk up Kardinal-Faulhaber-Strasse is one of Cuvilliés' finest works, the **Erzbischöfliches Palais** (Archbishop's Palace) at No. 7. Its ornate façade is a marvel of rococo stucco work.
From Promenadeplatz, you can reach two smart shopping streets, Maffeistrasse and Theatinerstrasse.

Residenz

RESIDENZ

On the north side of Max-Joseph-Platz, the Residenz was the Wittelsbachs' stronghold from 1385, when a citizens' revolt made them leave the Alter Hof for something more secure, till 1918, when Munich's workers occupied the palace and the Wittelsbachs were deposed.

Max-Joseph-Platz E 4–5
- U-Bahn, S-Bahn Marienplatz or Odeonsplatz
- Tram 19 Nationaltheater
- Bus 53 Odeonsplatz

The Tuscan-Renaissance loggia of the former **Palais Törring** was designed by Leo von Klenze, one of Munich's greatest 19th-century architects. Since 1834, the Palais has served as the city's main post office. The statue of a seated figure in the centre of the square depicts Max-Joseph, Bavaria's first king. The magnificent **National Theatre**, on the east side of the square, was completed in the style of a neoclassical Greek temple in 1818. Ravaged by fire in 1823, it was rebuilt by Klenze only to be destroyed in World War II. The post-war reconstruction was a remarkable success and the theatre reopened in all its former glory in 1963.

Residenzmuseum E 4
- U-Bahn, S-Bahn Marienplatz or Odeonsplatz
- Tram 19 Nationaltheater
- Bus 53 Odeonsplatz
- Max-Joseph-Platz 3
- Tel. 29 06 71
- Apr–mid-Oct daily 9 a.m.–6 p.m.; mid-Oct–March 10 a.m.–4 p.m.
- Free audioguides.
- A Kombi-Karte includes entrance to the Schatzkammer.

The oldest surviving part of the present Residenz, originally a medieval stronghold, dates from 1571, during the reign of Albrecht V. Successive rulers added to it constantly, commissioning the city's finest architects. More than 100 of the Residenz's main rooms now comprise the museum, which you can visit on two different tour routes, one in the morning and the other in the afternoon.

Rooms to look out for include the **Ahnengalerie** (Ancestral Gallery), a study in rococo extravagance designed by Joseph Effner and completed in 1731. It displays portraits of 121 Wittelsbach rulers, constituting an impressive family tree that has more than a touch of the fanciful about it.

The portrait gallery ends at the **Porcelain Cabinet**, which along with other adjoining rooms is packed with beautiful objects in

The four Bavarian lions on Residenzstrasse, opposite the yellow Theatinerkirche, are said to bring good luck if you rub their noses.

porcelain from Meissen, Sèvres and Wedgwood, as well as from Munich's own Nymphenburg factory.

From here you can proceed to the **Grottenhof**, a courtyard created for Wilhelm V by Friedrich Sustris in 1580. In the centre is the Perseus Fountain, sculpted in bronze by Hubert Gerhard.

Nearby, the barrel-vaulted **Antiquarium** stands as one of the great secular achievements of the Renaissance. It was built for Albrecht V in 1581 to house his library and collection of antiquities. The chamber, 69 m (226 ft) long, was originally much plainer than what we see today—the frescoes were added by Munich artist Peter Candid early in the next century. The lavishly ornate **Reiche Kapelle** was the private chapel of Maximilian I, who also commissioned the **Steinzimmer**, covered with allegorical paintings on themes devised by the Duke himself.

Upstairs, the **Kurfürstenzimmer** (Elector's Apartments) were designed by François de Cuvilliés between 1746 and 1763. The same architect was also responsible for the splendid rococo wall panelling

Residenz

and console tables of the **Reiche Zimmer** (State Rooms), which include the marvellous Grüne Galerie (Green Gallery).

Schatzkammer der Residenz E 4
- U-Bahn, S-Bahn Marienplatz or Odeonsplatz
- Tram 19 Nationaltheater
- Bus 53 Odeonsplatz
- Max-Joseph-Platz 3
- Same hours as Residenzmuseum

The Wittelsbachs' treasury rooms are not to be missed. This spectacular collection, founded by Duke Albrecht V in 1565, includes King Arnulf of Corinthia's jewel-encrusted altar ciborium made in AD 890 from beaten gold, a sapphire-studded cup of 1563, and a dazzling late-16th-century statue of St George and the Dragon, in which both protagonists are studded with rubies, emeralds and sapphires. Here, too, are the Bavarian Crown Jewels, acquired after Napoleon made Bavaria a kingdom in 1806.

Cuvilliés-Theater E 4
- U-Bahn, S-Bahn Marienplatz or Odeonsplatz
- Tram 19 Max Joseph-Platz
- Residenzstrasse 1
- Undergoing renovation until June 2008; tel. 29 06 72 13

From Residenzstrasse, turn into the palace's Kapellenhof (Chapel Court)—be sure to give one of the guardian lions a rub for good luck on the way—and continue through to the Brunnenhof (Fountain Court). François de Cuvilliés's masterpiece was originally in the southeast corner of the courtyard. It was rebuilt in its present location on the north side after being bombed in World War II. Luckily, all the interior furnishings had been removed for safekeeping, and the tiny, four-tiered interior is a perfectly intact rococo gem. It was once the private theatre of the Wittelsbachs. During its renovation, operas and concerts are held in other venues such as the Gärtnerplatztheater.

Staatliches Museum Ägyptischer Kunst E 4
- U-Bahn, S-Bahn Odeonsplatz
- Tram 19 Nationaltheater
- Entrance Hofgartenstrasse 1 near the obelisk
- Tues–Fri 9 a.m.–5 p.m.;
- Tues also 7 p.m.–9 p.m.;
- Sat and Sun 10 a.m.–5 p.m.
- Tel. 29 85 46

Overlooking the Hofgarten, the northern section of the Residenz contains a first-rate collection of ancient Egyptian works, including relief sculptures, gold jewellery, tombs, statues recovered from

Emperor Hadrian's palace and other antiquities from all the main periods of ancient Egyptian history.

Hofgarten E 4
- U-Bahn Odeonsplatz

The Italianate geometric design of the Hofgarten was created between 1613 and 1617 during the reign of Maximilian I. Its centrepiece, the green-domed Diana Temple, is topped by a statue representing Bavaria. There's a great view of the Theatinerkirche's towers and dome to the west. On the other side, the building with the early 20th-century cupola and two enormous modern glass wings is the **Bayerische Staatskanzlei** (Bavarian State Chancellery). The older part was once the Army Museum, and severely damaged by World War II bombing. It was given its modern look by the Bavarian government in 1993 only after fierce local opposition had been overcome.

Theatermuseum E 4
- U-Bahn Odeonsplatz
- Galeriestrasse 4a
- Tel 210 69 10

Around the edge of the Hofgarten, the 18th-century arcade has trendy art shops and galleries, a couple of elegant cafés and the Theatre Museum with a library (Tues and Thurs 10 a.m.– noon, 1.30–4 p.m.) and photo exhibitions (Tues 10 a.m.–noon, Thurs 2–4 p.m.). At the entrance, the Münchner Spielplan displays a vast panorama of Munich scenes (Tues–Fri 10 a.m.–4 p.m. Temporary exhibitions illustrate the life of the theatre and some of its great actors.

Theatinerkirche E 4
- U-Bahn Odeonsplatz
- Theatinerstrasse 22
- Mon–Sat 6.30 a.m.–7 p.m.;
- Sun 7.30 a.m.–7.30 p.m.
- Royal crypt: May–Nov Mon–Fri 10 a.m–1 p.m., 1.30–4.30 p.m., Sat 10 a.m.–3 p.m.

If you leave the Hofgarten by the southwest gate, you'll arrive on Odeonsplatz. Dominating the scene is the glorious Italian baroque façade of the Theatine Church (a religious order founded in 1524). It was commissioned to celebrate the birth of the Elector Max Emanuel in 1662 and designed by Agostino Barelli, though the final flourishes of the towers and gable were completed a century later by the rococo master François de Cuvilliés. Its richly decorated interior is ablaze with white and gold stucco work. The Fürstengruft (royal crypt) beneath the high altar contains the tombs of Max Emanuel, King Max I Joseph and other illustrious Wittelsbachs.

Behind the church, the **Theatinerhof** is an elegant courtyard with antique shops, boutiques and the refined Arzmiller tearoom.

Feldherrnhalle E 4
- U-Bahn Odeonsplatz

This grandiose 19th-century loggia is based on the late-Gothic Loggia dei Lanzi in Florence. Built by Friedrich von Gärtner for Ludwig I, the Field Marshal's Hall honours two generals who led Bavaria to victory on the battlefield: Count Johann Tilly, who distinguished himself during the Thirty Years' War, and Prince Karl-Philipp von Wrede, who fought against Napoleon in 1814. The plaque on the east side of the hall commemorates four policemen who died here in November 1923 when, during the Beer Hall Putsch, Hitler marched his stormtroopers up Residenzstrasse to defeat in a gun battle with the police.

Kunsthalle der Hypo-Kulturstiftung D 4
- U-Bahn Odeonsplatz
- Theatinerstrasse 8, Perusahof
- Daily 10 a.m.–8 p.m.
- Tel. 22 44 12
- www.hypo-kunsthalle.de

This popular art gallery puts on classy temporary exhibitions that cover the spectrum from stylish antiques to trendy avant-garde.

Maximilianstrasse E–F 5
- U-Bahn Odeonsplatz
- S-Bahn Marienplatz
- Tram 19 Nationaltheater

Starting at Max-Joseph-Platz, this impressive thoroughfare extends to the River Isar, beyond which you'll see the huge, neo-Renaissance **Maximilianeum**, commissioned by Maximilian II as a school for gifted students and now home to the Bavarian State Parliament. The Max II Monument, honouring the art-loving king, stands in the middle of Maximilianstrasse just before it reaches the river. Other landmarks include Bürklein's massive neo-Gothic Upper Bavarian Government building (1856–64), opposite the Ethnology Museum; the Vier Jahreszeiten (Four Seasons) hotel at No. 17; and across from it, the Kammerspiele theatre.

Staatliches Museum für Völkerkunde F 5
- U-Bahn Lehel
- S-Bahn Isartor
- Tram 17, 19 Max-Monument
- Maximilianstrasse 42
- Tues–Sun 9.30 a.m.–5.15 p.m.
- Tel. 21 01 36-100

The Ethnology Museum boasts a large collection of art and artefacts from Africa, Asia, Oceania and Latin America. Much of it was gathered by the Wittelsbachs.

KÖNIGSPLATZ

This area of monumental art galleries and neoclassical buildings northwest of the Altstadt is largely the brainchild of Ludwig I, whose obsession with classical Greece led to his desire to see Munich turned into an "Athens by the Isar". Two marvellous offshoots of this obsession were the Glyptothek and the Alte Pinakothek. A third remarkable outcome was that Ludwig's son, Otto, became the first king of independent Greece in 1832, and further fired up Bavarian enthusiasm for all things neoclassical.

Work on and around the square began under Leo von Klenze in 1816. By the 1930s, it had been paved for Hitler's army to parade on, and characterless new buildings were put up in the vicinity. Some of the Nazis' buildings were detonated after the war. The grass has been relaid, restoring something of its original appearance.

Propyläen C 3
- U-Bahn Königsplatz
- Königsplatz

Modelled on the Propylaeum, the temple entrance to the Acropolis in Athens, Klenze's Doric-style structure was only given the go-ahead by Ludwig the day after he abdicated in 1848. It's not really an entrance so much as a glorified screen blocking off the road behind. The pediment sculptures celebrate the victory of the Greeks in their war of independence against Turkey. This led to the accession of King Otto, who is also featured among them. Otto wasn't very popular with his subjects and was deposed in 1862, the year the Propyläen was completed.

Antikensammlungen C 4
- U-Bahn Königsplatz
- Königsplatz 1
- Tues, Thurs–Sun 10 a.m.–5 p.m., Wed to 8 p.m.
- Tel. 59 98 8 30

The Museum of Classical Art is on the south side of Königsplatz. Exemplifying the Corinthian order and looking like a Greek temple, it dates from Ludwig's fateful year of 1848. The building now houses an impressive collection of ancient Greek vases, pottery and bronzes, Etruscan artwork, and gold and silver ornaments, such as the gold funeral wreath of Armento.

Glyptothek C–D 3
- U-Bahn Königsplatz
- Königsplatz 3
- Tues–Sun 10 a.m.–5 p.m.; Thurs 10 a.m.–8 p.m.
- Tel. 28 61 00

Königsplatz

Across the square, Leo von Klenze gave the Glyptothek a magnificent portico of Ionic columns. It was built between 1816 and 1830 specifically for Ludwig I's personal collection of Greek and Roman sculptures. Among the many fine pieces is the famous *Barberini Faun,* a sculpture of a sleeping satyr from 220 BC that is so lifelike it looks as if he might wake at any moment. Pride of place, though, goes to the gables taken from the Temple of Aphaia on Aegina. The figures from the west gable date from around 500 BC, while those from the east are probably from 485–480 BC. Dominated by the central figure of Pallas Athene, they are highly stylized, yet with a wonderful sense of movement—firing arrows, falling in battle, muscles bulging with the effort. It's no surprise that they are almost as coveted by the Greek government as the Elgin Marbles.

Lenbachhaus C 3
- U-Bahn Königsplatz
- Luisenstrasse 33
- Tues–Sun, holidays 10 a.m.–6 p.m.
- Tel. 233 320 00

You can take a break from Ludwig's neoclassical landscape by walking

Refreshing relief from Königsplatz's symmetry in Lenbachhaus garden.

just behind the Propyläen to this Florentine-Renaissance style villa, built in 1891 for the society artist Franz von Lenbach (1836–1904). There are several of Lenbach's own works displayed in rooms decorated as the artist would have known them. He was extremely successful in his day as a portrait painter and produced around 80 of Bismarck alone. But these paintings pale somewhat in comparison to the rest of the collection, with its extensive section devoted to the Munich *Blaue Reiter* group, with canvasses by Kandinsky, Klee, Marc and Macke, together with several other powerful works by the German Expressionists.

The Lenbachhaus also puts on well-conceived and challenging temporary exhibitions of modern art, as does its sister institution, the **Lenbachhaus Kunstbau**, located below ground in the nearby Königsplatz U-Bahn station.

Paläontologisches Museum C 3

- U-Bahn Königsplatz
- Richard-Wagner-Strasse 10
- Mon–Thurs 8 a.m.–4 p.m.; Fri 8 a.m.–2 p.m.; first Sun in month 10 a.m.–4 p.m.
- Tel. 21 80 66 30

Behind the Lenbachhaus, this museum is packed with skeletons and other prehistoric mementos, including a 10 million-year-old elephant from Upper Bavaria and a crocodile which lived 190 million years ago in Baden-Württemberg.

Hochschule für Musik D 3

- U-Bahn Königsplatz
- Arcisstrasse 12
- For information on concerts call 28 92 74 42

From Königsplatz, turn left after the Glyptothek onto Arcisstrasse, and immediately on your right you will see the music academy building. Built in 1933 under the Nazi regime, at which time it was known as the Führerbau, its blockish colonnade is a rather grim architectural nod to the neoclassicism of the area.
The Hochschule is open these days for classical music concerts; in 1938 it was Hitler's Conference Building, where British Prime Minister Neville Chamberlain signed the notorious Munich Agreement, leading directly to the Nazi invasion of Czechoslovakia.

Karolinenplatz D 3

- U-Bahn Königsplatz
- Tram 27 Karolinenplatz

Head back to Brienner Strasse and follow the road left to Karolinenplatz, marked by a 29-m-high (95-ft) obelisk. The monument was made out of bronze melted

Königsplatz

down from Turkish cannons and ships sunk at the Battle of Navarino in 1827. Leo von Klenze designed it in honour of the 30,000 Bavarian soldiers who lost their lives in the disastrous 1812 Russian campaign.

Alte Pinakothek D 3

- U-Bahn Königsplatz
- Tram 27 Pinakothek
- Barer Strasse 27 (entrance on Theresienstrasse)
- Tues 10 a.m.–8 p.m., Wed–Sun 10 a.m.–7 p.m.
- Tel. 23 80 52 16

Leading north from Karolinenplatz, Barer Strasse is home to three of Germany's most important art galleries. The Alte Pinakothek ranks alongside the best in the world, with a magnificent collection of European art from the 14th to the 18th centuries. The paintings were collected by several generations of Wittlesbachs—King Ludwig I commissioned the vast Renaissance-style building from Leo von Klenze specifically in order to house them. There are great works in every room, but the early Flemish highlights include Rogier van der Weyden's detailed *Adoration of the Magi* triptych and self-referential *St Luke Painting the Virgin,* as well as Hans Memling's *The Seven Joys of Mary*. The German Renaissance section is dominated by Albrecht Dürer, notably the famous flowing golden locks of his *Self-Portrait* and the towering achievement of the late *Four Apostles*. Look out too for Matthias Grünewald's *Disputation of St Erasmus and St Maurice*, and Albrecht Altdorfer's *Battle of Alexander*, as teeming with extras as a Hollywood epic.

The Italian Renaissance is represented by a full squad of heavyweights—there are three exquisite Giotto altar panels on the theme of Christ's last days, an early Leonardo da Vinci *Madonna and Child,* paintings by Raphael and a superb collection of Titians, including *Christ Crowned with Thorns,* completed when the artist was 90. Baroque art is here in strength, with one of the world's great gatherings of works by Rubens, as well as contributions from Rembrandt, Van Dyck and Tiepolo.

Finish off with the roomful of Spanish paintings, with Velázquez, El Greco and the ever-popular beggar-boys depicted by Murillo.

Neue Pinakothek D 3

- U-Bahn Königsplatz
- Tram 27 Pinakothek
- Barer Strasse 29 (entrance on Theresienstrasse)
- Mon, Thurs–Sun 10 a.m.–5 p.m.; Wed 10 a.m.–8 p.m.
- Tel. 23 80 51 95

Sightseeing

The "New" gallery opened in 1981 on the site of another of Ludwig's grand projects, a gallery for 19th-century art that was destroyed during World War II. The multi-level modern interior is designed as a figure 8. In addition to a large group of 19th- and early 20th-century German works by artists such as Max Liebermann, Carl Spitzweg and Franz von Lenbach, you'll find some internationally known modern masters—the excellent French Impressionist room features three late Van Goghs, Manet's familiar *Breakfast in the Studio,* and canvases by Cézanne, Monet and Gauguin. Look out also for German Impressionists, such as Lovis Corvinth, and the stunning Jugendstil effect of Gustav Klimt's portrait of *Margarethe Stonborough-Wittgenstein.*

WELCOME CARD

Munich has a remarkable wealth of attractions, and visiting them all could easily deprive you of a considerable part of your own wealth. You can help matters by investing in the **München Welcome Card**. This gives up to 50% reductions at selected museums, cinemas, palaces, theatres, city tours and bicycle hire, plus free travel on public transport within the city limits. A single day ticket costs 7.50€, for three days it's 17.50€, while a Partner 1-Day card, valid for 5 people (two children of 6–14 years count as one adult) is 12.50€, for 3 days 25.50€ and on the whole network 48€. Cards are available at the main tourist offices, hotels, kiosks and department stores. An even cheaper alternative is to visit the old and new Pinakotheks, the Glyptotek, the Bavarian National Museum and the Museum of Egyptian Art on Sundays when entrance is 1€ and the Stadtmuseum free.

Pinakothek der Moderne D 3

- U-Bahn Königsplatz or Theresienstrasse
- Tram 27 Pinakothek
- Barer Strasse 40
- Tues, Wed, Sat, Sun 10 a.m.–5 p.m.;
- Thurs and Fri 10 a.m.–8 p.m.
- Tel. 23 80 53 60

This art gallery groups four museums: modern paintings, design, architecture and graphic works, covering trends in art up to the present day. The paintings include an impressive range of 20th-century works, among them Matisse, Kandinsky, Klee, Kirchner, Picasso and others—up to the more unconventional video installations of Pipilotti Rist. There are thousands of drawings and prints (Leonardo da Vinci, Cézanne, and so on), and over 50,000 objects illustrating the Applied Arts.

Schwabing

SCHWABING

Strictly speaking, the Schwabing district begins with Leopoldstrasse, north of the Siegestor, but any walk from the centre of town will naturally commence at Odeonsplatz and take in the handsome buildings along Ludwigstrasse. Schwabing is not really an area of museums and monuments, but rather one defined by a certain cultural ambience. In the years before and after World War I it was known as the Montmartre of Munich, a haunt of artists, writers and oddball Bohemians, such as the failed painter and would-be politician Adolf Hitler. That era has long since passed, but Schwabing still has enough of its atmospheric bars, cafés, galleries and bookshops to make a walk around its streets a fascinating experience.

Ludwigstrasse E 4–F 1
- U-Bahn Universität

Running from Odeonsplatz to the Siegestor, this great boulevard is another realisation of Ludwig I's dreams to transform the Bavarian capital into a city of royal dimensions. The palazzi at the southern end were designed by Leo von Klenze in Italian-Renaissance style.

Bayerische Staatsbibliothek E 3
- U-Bahn Universität
- Ludwigstrasse 16
- Daily 8 a.m.–midnight (general reading room).
- Tel. 28 63 82 32 2

The monumental Bavarian State Library, built by Friedrich von Gärtner in 1843, is the largest library in the German-speaking world. You can get into the general reading room and also see Duke Albrecht V's 16th-century globes of the earth and the heavens.

Ludwigskirche E 3
- U-Bahn Universität
- Ludwigstrasse
- Open daily 8 a.m.–7.30 p.m.

Commissioned by Ludwig and also built by von Gärtner, this handsome church is next door to the library. The façade is notable for its widely spaced neo-Romanesque towers, while the interior boasts an enormous ceiling fresco of the *Last Judgement* by Peter Cornelius, intended as both homage and rival to Michelangelo's masterpiece in the Sistine Chapel. Note also the prevailing architectural motif of *Rondbogenstil*, which dictates that round arches be used wherever possible. Cooked up by Ludwig and von Gärtner, this style also dominates the university buildings, just to the north. Opposite the church is the entrance to Schellingstrasse, one of the liveliest streets in this student neighbourhood.

Ludwig-Maximilians Universität E 2–3

- U-Bahn Universität
- Geschwister-Scholl-Platz 1

The university occupies both sides of Ludwigstrasse. It's now one of the three biggest universities in Germany, with some 46,000 students and 800 lecturers. It has attracted many distinguished academics, including Röntgen, who discovered the X-ray, and Ohm, who gave his name to units of electrical resistance.

Just as admirable were Hans and Sophie Scholl, the brother and sister who founded the White Rose movement in the 1930s to resist the Nazis, and paid for it with their lives. A memorial to them can be seen just beyond the university's entrance hall (Mon–Fri 10 a.m.–4 p.m.; guided tours tel. 21 89 53 59).

Siegestor E 2

- U-Bahn Universität
- Ludwigstrasse

The large Victory Gate (1843–52) marks the end of Ludwigstrasse. It was commissioned by Ludwig I not just as a piece of neoclassical imperial pomp—it's based on the Constantine Gate in Rome—but as a sop to the Bavarian army, in whose honour it was erected. The gate was damaged during the war and has been left bearing its scars as a comment on the dangers of militarism; the inscription on the south side translates "Dedicated to victory, destroyed in war, exhorting peace".

Around Leopoldstrasse E 1–2

- U-Bahn Universität, Giselastrasse or Münchener Freiheit

Heading north from Siegestor, Leopoldstrasse is Schwabing's main artery, and pulses with life day and night. This long, broad, tree-lined avenue is often referred to as Munich's Champs-Elysées, and with its many pavement cafés, bars, ice-cream parlours and fashionable boutiques, it's easy to see why. On warm Sunday afternoons it becomes a favourite promenade for locals and visitors alike, at which time the outdoor cafés are very much the places to see and be seen. Immediately on the left after the Siegestor, the **Akademie der Bildenden Künste** (Academy of Fine Arts) was built in Venetian Renaissance style in 1887. Many famous artists studied here, including Wassily Kandinsky and Paul Klee, members of the *Blaue Reiter* group, and in the 1890s its

Schwabing

students spearheaded the Jugendstil (Art Nouveau) movement.
Further up, on the right, you can't miss the gigantic **Walking Man**, made by American sculptor Jonathan Borofsky for the Münchener Rückversicherung insurance company.
For a flavour of old Schwabing, you need to duck along some of the side streets off Leopoldstrasse. Halfway up, **Ainmillerstrasse** contains fine examples of Jugendstil architecture. See, on the façade of No. 22, Adam and Eve at the base of the Tree of Knowledge. The street was home to Klee (No. 32), the poet Rainer Maria Rilke (No. 34) and Kandinsky. Parallel **Hohenzollernstrasse** also has many Jugendstil buildings; it is the district's best shopping street with dozens of quirky fashion boutiques.
Wedekindplatz (F 1) at the end of Feilitzschstrasse, was once the centre of Schwabing's rollicking cabaret and theatre scene, and is still the district's focal point. Werneckstrasse starting in the southwest corner, and Nikolaiplatz retain the charms of the area's early 20th-century heyday.

Five storeys high, the Walking Man seems all set to explore the delights of Leopoldstrasse.

Sightseeing

ENGLISCHER GARTEN

Schwabing's eastern neighbour is the vast Englischer Garten. It extends for almost 5 km (3 miles) northwards, making it one of the biggest as well as loveliest city parks in the world. It's an unbeatable place for strolling, picnicking, sunbathing, or simply taking time out from the bustle of the city, before or after a visit to the nearby museums and galleries.

Englischer Garten F 1–3
U-Bahn Münchener Freiheit
The park was laid out between 1789 and 1793 by Count Rumford, who began life as plain Benjamin Thompson. He was an American who sided with the British during the War of Independence and left after they were defeated. The name comes from the contemporary fashion for a more informal, "natural" landscape following the English model, as opposed to the strict patterning of the French style. It's also no accident that work on the park began in the same year as the French Revolution, as it was intended by Rumford and the Elector Karl Theodor to provide employment and take Müncheners' minds off the unsettling subject of France.

Entering the park from the roads leading east from the U-Bahn, you will soon see the **Kleinhesseloher See**, a glorious little lake packed with swans and geese. Take a boat out onto the water or, if you're less energetically inclined, have a drink at the lakeside restaurant.
If you follow the fast-flowing Eisbach river south for a short distance and then turn in towards the centre of the park, you'll soon come to one of Munich's most popular beer gardens at the **Chinesischer Turm** (Chinese Tower), a pagoda dating originally from 1789 and reconstructed after suffering serious war damage.
Just south of here is the **Monopteros**, a small neoclassical temple designed by Leo von Klenze. Its location on a man-made hill gives it a fine sweeping view of the city's spires and domes. In summer, the meadow by the Eisbach near here becomes a popular sunbathing spot for FKK enthusiasts—the German acronym for *Freikörperkultur*—nudism.
It's a short walk from here down past the Japanese Tea House and onto Prinzregentenstrasse. At the southern boundary of the park, this is one of Munich's most exclusive addresses, with a couple of museums that should not be missed.

Englischer Garten

The garden is English, the tower Chinese, but the beer is 100 per cent German.

Bayerisches Nationalmuseum F 4
- U-Bahn Lehel
- Tram 17 or Bus 100 Nationalmuseum/Haus der Kunst
- Prinzregentenstrasse 3
- Tues–Sun 10 a.m.–5 p.m.; Thurs to 8 p.m.
- Tel. 21 12 40 1

This huge collection is devoted mainly to Bavarian and German art and folklore. It was begun under Maximilian II in 1855, although the building dates from 1900 during the rule of Prince Regent Luitpold. The museum contains many remarkable works spanning the early medieval and Gothic periods through to Art Nouveau. Look out in particular for the sublime carvings of Tilman Riemenschneider (1460–1531), whose figures such as the Twelve Apostles, St Barbara and St Sebastian rank among the greatest achievements of late Gothic German art. There are some superb artefacts by medieval German goldsmiths, paintings by Renaissance masters including Holbein and Cranach, an alabaster statue of Judith and Holofernes by Conrad Meit and everything from ancient armour and weaponry to Albrecht V's dinner service. Not to be missed is Jakob Sandtner's detailed wooden model of Munich, made in 1572. Be sure also to seek out the fine collection of traditional Bavarian and Tyrolean crèches, as well as other folkloric items from around the region, located in the basement.

Archäologische Staatssammlung F 4
- U-Bahn Lehel
- Tram 17 or Bus 100
- Nationalmuseum/Haus der Kunst
- Lerchenfeldstrasse 2
- Tues–Sun 9 a.m.–4.30 p.m.
- Tel. 21 12 40 2

This collection of pre- and ancient history displays archaeological items found in Bavaria and dating from the Stone and Bronze ages up to the foundation of Munich in the 12th century. The collection of objects from the Celtic and Roman eras are especially noteworthy, and bring to life aspects of Munich's earliest history.

Schack-Galerie F 4
- U-Bahn Odeonsplatz or Lehel
- Bus 100 Reitmorstrasse
- Prinzregentenstrasse 9
- Wed–Sun 10 a.m.–5 p.m.
- Tel. 23 80 52 24

Continuing along Prinzregentenstrasse, you'll come to the former Prussian embassy on the corner of Oettingenstrasse. It now contains the legacy of Count Schack, a Prussian official who amassed a large collection of 19th-century German art. It is strongly weighted towards German Romanticism, with paintings by Carl Spitzweg, Franz von Lenbach, Arnold Böcklin and Anselm Feuerbach.

Haus der Kunst F 4
- U-Bahn Odeonsplatz or Lehel
- Tram 17 or Bus 100
- Nationalmuseum/Haus der Kunst
- Prinzregentenstrasse 1
- Open daily 10 a.m.–8 p.m.
- Tel. 21 12 71 13

The large, colonnaded Haus der Kunst was opened by Hitler in 1937 as the House of German Art, an event celebrated by the notorious exhibition of "Depraved Art". This showed works by artists such as Klee, Kandinsky and Chagall, which were intended to be the subject of ridicule by the Nazis. While these paintings have come to be regarded as modern masterpieces, the propagandist art favoured by Hitler has long been consigned to history's rubbish bin. The collection has now moved to a new home in the Pinakothek der Moderne. The Haus der Kunst still functions as a gallery of contemporary art, and as a theatre for the Bayerisches Staatsschauspiel.

HAIDHAUSEN

Lying across the River Isar, Haidhausen first developed around the bridge put up by Henry the Lion in the 12th century to cash in on the salt trade with Salzburg, and is thus the oldest part of the city outside the Altstadt. By the 19th century, it was a poor working-class district, and remained run-down well into the 20th century. One thing it always possessed, however, was a lively, earthy character, something which continues to this day despite the area's increasing gentrification since the 1980s. This is where Munich's Bohemian set moved when Schwabing became too expensive, and it can now boast the city's trendiest nightlife and entertainment. Here, too, is the Gasteig arts complex, opened in 1985, making Haidhausen an important centre of highbrow culture as well.

Friedensengel G 4
- U-Bahn Prinzregentenstrasse
- Bus 100 Prinzregentenplatz
- Prinzregentenstrasse

The shining Angel of Peace looks back down Prinzregentenstrasse from her Corinthian column in celebration of 25 years of peace following the Franco-Prussian war of 1871. But based on Athena Nike, Winged Victory, and with sculptures of Bismarck, the Kaiser and Moltke, the German general, the angel clearly has far more to do with the success of war than the benefits of peace.

Villa Stuck G 4
- U-Bahn Prinzregentenstrasse
- Tram 18/Bus 100 Friedensengel
- Prinzregentenstrasse 60
- Tues–Sun 11 a.m.–6 p.m.
- Tel. 45 55 51 45

Carry on past the Friedensengel to the splendid Jugendstil palace of the painter Franz von Stuck, dating from 1897–98. The interior mosaics, frescoes, gold and green decor and Stuck's own paintings encapsulate all the classic elements of the Jugendstil movement. The equestrian statue of *Amazone* outside was cast to a design by Stuck in 1913–14.

Around Haidhausen F–G 5–6
- U-Bahn Max-Weber-Platz
- Tram 18 Max-Weber-Platz

The area around Villa Stuck is at the southern end of the upmarket Bogenhausen district. For a change of tempo, head down through leafy, riverside **Maximilianpark** to the heart of Haidhausen.

You can get a good flavour of the quarter by making for **Wiener Platz**. Dominated by the massive

Hofbräukeller, one of Munich's finest old beer cellars, and with a boisterous daily food market, the square retains the earthy character of Haidhausen's working-class past, while also having its fair share of new, trendy bistros and bars. Behind here, on Johannisplatz, you'll find the attractive, red-brick **Johanniskirche**, built in 1874 and known familiarly as Haidhausen's Cathedral. Nearby Preysingstrasse has a remarkable timber-framed house which survives from the 17th century at no 71. From here you can walk westwards to the monumental Gasteig arts centre on the corner of Rosenheimer Strasse, one of Haidhausen's liveliest streets. Over by the River Isar, **Müller'sches Volksbad** is a marvellous Jugendstil swimming baths built in 1901. The interior has beautiful stucco work, and there's a pleasant café.

Deutsches Museum E 6
- U-Bahn Fraunhoferstrasse
- S-Bahn Isartor
- Tram 18 Deutsches Museum
- Museumsinsel 1
- Daily 9 a.m.–5 p.m.; closed on certain holidays
- Tel. 21 79 1

On an island in the Isar, just south of Ludwigsbrücke (Ludwig's Bridge), is one of the world's largest museums of science and technology, with an interesting department of atomic and nuclear physics and a genetics laboratory. Its size can seem daunting— 55,000 sq m (66,000 sq yd) of exhibition space covering seven floors—but the hands-on, user-friendly approach makes it a fairly easy-going as well as fascinating lesson in what makes the modern world tick. There's a superb collection of early cars, including an 1886 Benz and the streamlined aluminium BMW Wendler of 1938; bi-planes that once belonged to the Wright brothers and Blériot; and displays on steam locomotives, submarines, rockets, aeronautics, turbines and so on. Guided tours of the vintage car repair workshop on request. The interactive exhibits are sure to appeal to children, as is the labyrinthine and realistic recreation of a coal mine in the basement.

forum am deutschen museum E 6
- S-Bahn Isartor
- Tram 18 Deutsches Museum
- Museumsinsel 1
- Daily 9 a.m.–11 p.m.
- Tl. 21 12 52 00

Three cinemas using state-of-the-art techniques, and among them one with Germany's biggest digital screen. Also changing exhibitions on various cultural themes.

Around Munich

AROUND MUNICH

Some of Munich's most outstanding sights are just beyond the city centre. Indeed, places as varied as the Wittelsbachs' summer palace, the site of the Oktoberfest and the Dachau Concentration Camp memorial are integral to any understanding of Munich's complex history. What's more, all of them are easily reached by train or tram.

Schloss Nymphenburg

- Tram 17 Schloss Nymphenburg; Bus 51 Schloss Nymphenburg
- Palace and Amalienburg daily April–mid-Oct 9 a.m.–6 p.m.; mid-Oct–Mar 10 a.m.–4 p.m.
- Pagodenburg, Badenburg and Magdalenenklause summer only, 9 a.m.–6 p.m.
- Park open in summer 6 a.m.–9.30 p.m.; restricted hours rest of year.

Like the Theatinerkirche, the Nymphenburg Palace was built to an Agostino Barelli design for Princess Henriette Adelaide, following the birth of Max Emanuel in 1662. It was originally a relatively modest summer villa, but when he later became Elector, Max Emanuel had the north and south wings added, and over successive generations, pavilions, lodges and the superbly laid-out gardens transformed it into a palace on the grand scale. You can visit the various parts separately, although it's better value to buy a combined ticket, as nothing is worth missing. The palace has a magnificent central baroque banqueting hall, with an enormous ceiling fresco showing the Goddess Flora and her nymphs. There are some delightful rooms leading off from here, such as Max Emanuel's tapestry room, but the undoubted winner is the Schönheitsgalerie. This contains the portraits of 36 beautiful women who caught the eye of Ludwig I, including the dark-eyed Lola Montez, née Eliza Gilbert from Limerick in Ireland. Ludwig lost his heart to Lola, and eventually his crown as well, when Munich citizens tired of his extravagant behaviour with her and deposed him in 1848.

The **Marstallmuseum**, in the former royal stables in the south wing, has a dazzling array of ornate carriages and sleighs which belonged to the Wittelsbachs. Karl Albrecht's baroque coronation coach was made in Paris in 1730, but even this cannot compete with Ludwig II's wonderland Nymph Sleigh and his carriage that looks like something from a Baron von Münchhausen fantasy. Upstairs is

the **Porcelain Museum**, with a collection of Nymphenburg porcelain from the nearby factory. The **Schlosspark** is a great place for a stroll. Dotted around it are some fine buildings put up for the amusement of the Wittelsbachs. Pride of place goes to the **Amalienburg**, a perfect pink and white rococo confection designed by François de Cuvilliés as a hunting lodge. Note the kennels built into the walls of the reception room; above them are the gun cabinets. The main circular Hall of Mirrors is a marvel of rococo decoration, its blue and silver walls covered with hunting motifs and stucco cherubs and nymphs. It's also worth seeking out the **Badenburg**, the Wittelsbachs' heated indoor swimming pool built by Joseph Effner in 1721 complete with a baroque banqueting hall; and the **Kascade**, a waterfall surrounded by statues, with a vista along a canal to the palace.

Olympia Park

- U-Bahn Olympiazentrum
- Tower open daily 9 a.m.–midnight (last entry 11.30 p.m.)

The park was laid out for the 1972 Olympic Games. Dominating the

Nymphenburg park attracts flocks of visitors.

scene is the 290-m (950-ft) **Olympiaturm** (Olympic Tower), which offers panoramic views and a revolving restaurant (daily 11 a.m.–5 p.m. and 6.30 p.m.–midnight). The buildings are very much a 1970s vision of futuristic architecture. The Olympia-Schwimmhalle is a public swimming pool. The **Theatron**, on the Olympic lake, puts on free open-air rock concerts in summer. On the other side of the lake, the steep **Olympiaberg** has a good view over the park—it was built out of the rubble collected from buildings bombed during the war. The top names in rock, jazz, international folklore and action theatre get together for the annual Tollwood Festival.

BMW Museum Zeithorizont

- U-Bahn Olympiazentrum
- Petuelring 130
- Closed for renovation until 2007.

The collections of the museum—a large metallic capsule located in front of the striking four-cylinder BMW tower—can be seen during the renovation at the Olympiaturm, Spiridon-Louis-Ring 7. There are enough vintage cars, Formula 1 racers and motorbikes to keep the most technophobic visitors interested.

Sightseeing

Gedenkstätte Dachau
- S-Bahn Dachau, then bus 726
- Alte Römerstrasse 75
- Tues–Sun 9 a.m.–5 p.m.
- Film shown in English at 11.30 a.m. and 3.30 p.m.

Out to the northwest of Munich, this was Nazi Germany's first concentration camp. From 1933 it housed many different victims of the regime's brutal paranoia, including political opponents, Jews, Gypsies and homosexuals—up to 32,000 people were killed here. A permanent exhibition, documentary film and the grim, powerful aura of the camp itself amount to a harrowing yet vitally important testament of Munich's darkest days. While you are here, take time to look around the town itself, which carefully tends its picturesque historic centre and lively cultural scene around a grand castle of the Wittelbachs.

Theresienwiese B 6
- U-Bahn Theresienwiese

This vast area west of the Altstadt is famously home to the October beer festival, when it becomes a riot of beer tents, beer drinkers, funfairs and parades in traditional costume. The rest of the year it's a pretty forlorn open space that is most remarkable for an enormous bronze statue of *Bavaria* (with a panoramic view of the town from its head, daily in summer 9 a.m.–6 p.m.), and Leo von Klenze's neoclassical Ruhmeshalle (Hall of Fame), completed in 1853 and containing the busts of over 70 important Bavarians.

Hellabrunn Zoo
- U-Bahn Thalkirchen Zoo
- Bus 52 Flamingoeingang
- Tierparkstrasse 30
- Open Apr–Sep 8 a.m.–6 p.m.;
- Oct–Mar 9 a.m.–5 p.m.

The zoo dates from 1911, although it was turned into the world's first "Geo-Zoo" in 1928, when animals were grouped together by region of origin. This layout is still in place, and today the Hellabrunn is reputed to be one of the world's more enlightened zoos. There are animals from all the continents here, including some very rare breeds such as armoured rhinoceros, tarpan and white-tailed gnu. There's a popular children's zoo as well, where animals can be petted and fed.

Bavaria Filmstadt
- U-Bahn Wettersteinplatz or Silberhornstrasse
- Tram 25 Silberhornstrasse
- Bavariafilmplatz 7, Geiselgasteig
- March–Nov daily 9 a.m.–4 p.m.;
- Nov–Feb daily 10 a.m.–3 p.m.

Around Munich

guided tours several times an hour in summer, on the hour in winter. Information and booking: tel. 64 99 20 00

Germany's answer to Hollywood is at the centre of the nation's film and television industry. Tremendous fun even if you can't claim to be a dedicated fan of German soap opera. Tours take you through the sets of such blockbusters as *Das Boot*—the WWII epic set on a U-boat—*Cabaret* and *Marienhof*, popular TV series. You can watch stuntmen in action (March to December) or see a film in 3 or 4-D.

OKTOBERFEST

The Oktoberfest dates back to the marriage in October 1810 of Crown Prince Ludwig, the future King Ludwig I, and Princess Thérèse of Saxe-Hildburghausen. A huge folk festival was held to celebrate the event, which took place on a meadow west of the city. The area was later rechristened Theresienwiese in honour of the princess, though locals soon shortened this to "d'Wies'n". The party proved such a success that the good citizens of Munich decided to repeat it every year. It's now the biggest and most famous festival of its kind in the world, attracting around 7 million visitors from as far afield as Australia, the United States and Japan.

For 16 days, the Theresienwiese is transformed into a vast festival city, with huge beer tents put up by the main Munich breweries. These each house 6,000 drinkers, who sit on long benches and quaff beer by the litre *(Maas)* or, less often, the half litre *(eine Halbe)*, brought by impressively strong waitresses in traditional garb clutching up to ten enormous beer mugs at a time. Over the course of the festival, more than 6 million litres of beer and 200,000 pairs of pork sausages will go down the hatch, a guarantee that the tents are always boisterous and in the main highly convivial.

Outside, meanwhile, there is endless entertainment to relieve revellers of the money not spent on beer—food stalls, fairground rides, a giant Ferris wheel. The festival's opening Saturday begins with a Brewer's Parade, with marching brass bands and horse-drawn floats. The next day, there's a great costume procession of musicians, jesters and folklore groups. On the second Saturday, a concert of all the Oktoberfest bands is held at the *Bavaria* statue at 11 a.m.

Accommodation is scarce and expensive during the festival, so try to book a room as far in advance as possible. Dates for the upcoming Oktoberfests are 16 Sept–3 Oct 2006, 22 Sept–7 Oct 2007 and 20 Sept–5 Oct 2008.

Sightseeing

EXCURSIONS

For a wider view of Bavaria, why not take a day trip out to the lakes, castles and mountains of the Upper Bavarian countryside? Many of them can be reached by train from Munich. Alternatively, there are regular bus tours that take in all the main sights.

ROYAL CASTLES

At the foot of the Alps southwest of Munich is a set of extravagant 19th-century castles associated with the tragic King Ludwig II. He practically bankrupted the Bavarian exchequer in building them, and they certainly gave weight to the accusation of madness that pre-empted his downfall and subsequent death. It's not without irony that today their fantastic appearance and romantic legend make them some of Bavaria's biggest money-spinning tourist attractions.

Neuschwanstein

Perched on a forested hilltop overlooking a lake and with spectacular views across to the Alps, Ludwig's best-known madcap enterprise is the epitome of a fairytale castle. It's little wonder that the white granite walls and fanciful turreted towers were the inspiration for the centrepiece Cinderella castle at every Disneyland the world over. Building began in 1869, but the castle was still incomplete at the time of Ludwig's death in 1886.

Ludwig's greatest passion was music, and Neuschwanstein's neo-Gothic design pays homage to the medieval German bards who held singing contests at Wartburg Castle in Thuringia. The interior, however, honours Ludwig's contemporary musical hero, Richard Wagner. The superb Sängersaal (Minstrels' Hall) is decorated with sculptures and frescoes evoking scenes from Wagner's operas such as *Tannhäuser* and *Die Meistersinger von Nürnberg*. Tours also take you through the Throne Room, royal bed chamber and a lurid artificial grotto.

Hohenschwangau

Further down the road is another neo-Gothic pile, though this one was the brainchild of Ludwig's father, Maximilian II. Wagner was a guest here and played on the square-shaped piano in the Hohenstaufensaal. Ludwig's main legacy was the addition of lights in

Ludwig's fantasy of a knightly fortress at Neuschwanstein proved to be his swan song.

Sightseeing

his bedroom ceiling to make it resemble the night sky.

Linderhof

About 20 km (12 miles) east of Hohenschwangau, you find Ludwig in baroque mode. This delightful palace was the only one of his to be completed. It's based on the Grand Trianon at Versailles and testament to his deep admiration for Louis XIV.

The palace's interior is richly decorated in the baroque style, with plenty of stucco work and gold-painted ornamentation on display. The highlight is the Schlosspark, however, where the terraces and pools merge magically into the surrounding Alpine forests, while features such as the Venus Grotto—a reference to the first act of Tannhäuser—and the amazing Moorish Pavilion, purchased by Ludwig at the 1876 Paris World Fair, are reminders that the king's eccentric side was ever present.

THE LAKES

There's nothing more guaranteed to gladden a Bavarian's heart than to escape the city for one of the region's romantic Alpine lakes. The lakes fan out south of Munich and with their deep-blue water and Alpine backdrop offer some of Germany's most scenic landscapes.

Ammersee

S-Bahn Herrsching

Herrsching, a resort on the eastern side of the Ammersee, is a

---

THE PASSION AT OBERAMMERGAU

Unlikely as it may seem, the world's longest-running play is performed every ten years in a small village in the foothills of the Bavarian Alps. The *Passionsspiele* (Passion Play) was first acted by the villagers of Oberammergau after the Black Death had struck in 1633, and was the result of a pact with God—if He kept the plague away, they would continue to stage this dramatic portrayal of the death and resurrection of Christ. Both sides of the bargain were kept. Today, the cast is still made up of amateur actors from the village. For an extra touch of authenticity, they must refrain from having haircuts for several months before the performance. The play lasts a gruelling eight hours (including a three-hour lunchbreak) and runs from May to October. The most recent season was in 2000, and the next will be in 2010. As this deeply religious play reaches its 400th anniversary, its power to attract audiences is as strong as ever.

Excursions

lovely spot from which to set off on walks along the lake, or you can have a cooling swim at some of the nearby beaches in summer.

A popular trip from here is to head up Heiliger Berg (Holy Mountain) to the Benedictine abbey at **Andechs**. The original Gothic church was built to house holy relics brought from Jerusalem, but the current rococo form dates from the mid-18th century and is the work of Johann Baptist Zimmermann. Other pilgrims come for the famous Andechs beer brewed by the monks, which can be sampled in the adjacent Klosterbrauerei.

Starnberger See
: S-Bahn Starnberg

This lake, 20 km (12 miles) long, is a mere 30-minute ride southwest of Munich. At Starnberg you can pick up a boat for a three-hour mini-cruise, or shorter trips in fine weather. The town also has an attractive rococo parish church, whose high altar is by Ignaz Günther. The Starnberger See was once a pleasure ground for the Wittelsbachs and it was to **Schloss Berg** on the eastern shore that King Ludwig II was sent after being declared insane in 1886. Soon afterwards he drowned in the lake in mysterious circumstances. A memorial chapel was built at Berg in 1900 in his honour, while a nearby cross marks the spot where his body was found.

Chiemsee
: Train to Prien am Chiemsee

Around 50 km (30 miles) southeast of Munich, this beautiful lake is the largest in the region. From the charming main resort of Prien, you can take a 19th-century steam train to the harbour, where boats leave for trips around the lake and, more importantly, to Herreninsel, a small island that is home to Ludwig II's most ambitious project. **Schloss Herrenchiemsee** is his attempt at fully recreating Louis XIV's palace of Versailles. It was begun in 1878, and when work stopped eight years later, only a part of it was complete. The tour takes in the state rooms, including his never less than fascinating taste in bedchambers, although the undoubted highlight is the copy of Versailles's Hall of Mirrors. There's also a König-Ludwig-II-Museum, containing memorabilia relating to the king. If you have time, head over to **Fraueninsel**, another picturesque little island. Here you'll discover a fine 12th-century Romanesque church. You can also seek out the Torhalle, a 9th-century Carolingian gatehouse with a frescoed chapel.

Dining Out

Munich's dual role as Bavarian capital and cosmopolitan metropolis means that diners can enjoy the best of both worlds—good, hearty regional dishes at traditional *Gaststätten*, and top-quality Italian, French and other international cuisine in numerous speciality restaurants around town.

The following recommendations are marked with the € sign to give some idea of what you might expect to pay per head for a three-course meal excluding drinks:

€ budget price, €€ around 20–35€, €€€ more than 35€

ALTSTADT

Andechser am Dom
- U-Bahn, S-Bahn Marienplatz
- Weinstrasse 7
- Tel. 29 84 81
- Open daily 10 a.m.–1 a.m.

Right behind the Frauenkirche, this low-ceilinged bar-restaurant is a popular haunt with Munich's city-slickers and tourists alike. Good Bavarian cuisine and delicious Andechser monastery beer. €

Augustiner Gaststätte
- U-Bahn, S-Bahn Karlsplatz
- Neuhauser Strasse 27
- Tel. 23 18 32 57
- Restaurant open daily 10 a.m.–midnight;
- beer hall Mon–Sat 9 a.m.– midnight, Sun from 10 a.m.

The Augustiner is part restaurant, part beer hall, with a cavernous interior, traditional decor, long benches and even longer menu. It's a good place to try the Munich speciality of *Schweinhaxe* (grilled pork knuckles) with *Kartoffelknödel* (grated potato dumpling). €

Bayerischer Hof Garden Restaurant
- U-Bahn, S-Bahn Marienplatz
- Tram 19 Theatinerstrasse
- Promenadeplatz 2–6
- Tel. 2 12 09 93
- Open daily noon–3 p.m. and 6 p.m.–11.30 p.m.

Superb service and fine regional and international cuisine are the order of the day at this top-notch restaurant located inthe classy Bayerischer Hof Hotel. €€€

Bohne & Malz
- U-Bahn Sendlinger Tor or Karlsplatz

Dining Out

- Tram 17, 18, 19, 27
- Sonnenstrasse 11, entrance on Herzogspitalstrasse
- Tel. 55 71 79
- Daily 10 a.m.–1 a.m.

Modern, comfortable café serving international dishes, many kinds of coffee and beers. Perfect for a break while you're shopping. €€

bux

- U-Bahn Marienplatz
- Frauenstrasse 9
- Tel. 2 91 95 50
- Mon–Fri 11 a.m.–8.45 p.m.; Sat 11 a.m.–3 p.m.; closed Sun and holidays

Modern self-service café with generous salad buffet, ideal for vegetarians. €€

Café Glockenspiel

- U-Bahn, S-Bahn Marienplatz
- Marienplatz 28
- Tel. 26 42 56
- Mon–Sat 10 a.m.–1 a.m.; Sun and holidays 10 a.m.–7 p.m.

International and Bavarian cuisine overlooking Marienplatz, plus of course a ringside seat for the Town Hall's Glockenspiel show. € €€

Donisl

- U-Bahn, S-Bahn Marienplatz
- Weinstrasse 1
- Tel. 29 62 64
- Open 9 a.m.–midnight

The large and lively Donisl is a trusty old *Gaststätte* handily located next to Marienplatz. It's also great value. €

Haxnbauer im Scholastikerhaus

- U-Bahn, S-Bahn Marienplatz
- Sparkassenstrasse 6
- Tel. 21 66 54-0
- Daily 11 a.m.–midnight

A very traditional Bavarian inn, where mouth-watering aromas fill the air, courtesy of huge sides of pork and veal roasting over open beech-wood fires. €€

Hofer – Der Stadtwirt

- U-Bahn Marienplatz
- Burgstrasse 5
- Tel. 24 21 04 44
- Mon–Sat 10 a.m.–1 a.m.; Sun and holidays 10 a.m.–5 p.m.

Historic restaurant in a protected patrician house with inner courtyard and vaulted cellar. Bavarian and Austrian dishes in 1960s and 70s style. €€

Hundskugel

- U-Bahn, S-Bahn Marienplatz
- Hotterstrasse 18
- Tel. 26 42 72
- Open daily 10.30 a.m.–midnight

Munich's oldest inn dates from around 1440. The fine regional cuisine has a light touch, by

Tuck into bangers and mash, with sauerkraut, of course, at the Hofbräuhaus.

Bavarian standards, and the atmosphere is convivial. €

Hunsingers Pacific
U-Bahn, S-Bahn Karlsplatz
Maximiliansplatz 5
Tel. 55 02 97 41
Mon–Fri noon–3 p.m., 6 p.m.– 1 a.m.; Sat 6.30 p.m.–1 a.m.
The chef combines French cuisine with Asian, Oriental and Pacific flavours. Attentive service. €€

Nürnberger Bratwurst-Glöckl am Dom
U-Bahn, S-Bahn Marienplatz
Frauenplatz 9
Tel. 29 52 64
Mon–Sat 10 a.m.–1 a.m.; Sun and holidays 11 a.m.–11 p.m.
They've been serving up wholesome regional dishes at this atmospheric old restaurant next to the Dom for more than a century. Nuremberg-style Wurst (sausage) is the house speciality, served on pewter plates, but you'll come again for the succulent *Spanferkerl in Dunkelbier* (roast suckling pig in dark beer sauce). No menu. €–€€

Prinz Myshkin
U-Bahn, S-Bahn Marienplatz
Hackenstrasse 2

Dining Out

- Tel. 26 55 96
- Open daily 11 a.m.–1 a.m. Hot dishes served non-stop.

Probably the most highly regarded vegetarian spot in town. Its creative cooking calls on Asian and Italian influences; sushi, good pizzas, pasta and salads. €

Ratskeller

- U-Bahn, S-Bahn Marienplatz
- Marienplatz 8
- Tel. 2 19 98 90
- Open daily 10 a.m.–midnight

Located in the vast cellar beneath the Town Hall, this restaurant has a seemingly endless array of rooms, so it shouldn't be difficult finding a table here if everywhere else is busy. The service can be a little brusque, but the regional dishes are well prepared and always tasty. €€

Weisses Brauhaus im Tal

- U-Bahn, S-Bahn Marienplatz
- Im Tal 7
- Tel. 29 98 75
- Sun–Thurs 7 a.m.–1 a.m.;
- Fri, Sat 7 a.m.–3 a.m.

Big, rumbustious, and with a portrait of King Ludwig II watching over the proceedings, this is one of Munich's great beer halls. It serves excellent Bavarian cuisine, while the award-winning Schneider Weissbier is a feast in itself. €

Zum Spöckmeier am Roseneck

- U-Bahn, S-Bahn Marienplatz
- Rosenstrasse 9
- Tel. 26 80 88
- Mon–Sat 9.30 a.m.–midnight;
- Sun from 10 a.m.

A spacious, traditional *Gaststätte*, with outdoor seating on Rosenstrasse. It has an extensive *Wurst* menu—this is another noted spot for a pre-noon *Weisswurst*—as well as a wide range of toothsome cold dishes. €

RESIDENZ

Austernkeller Seafood Restaurant

- U-Bahn Marienplatz or Odeonsplatz
- S-Bahn Marienplatz
- Stollbergstrasse 11
- Tel. 29 87 87
- Open daily 5–1 a.m.

Award-winning restaurant. Oysters and seafood flown in straight from the sea. Limited wine list, but the prices are reasonable and the service professional. €€€

Café Roma

- U-Bahn Marienplatz or Odeonsplatz
- S-Bahn Marienplatz
- Tram 19
- Maximilianstrasse 31

Tel. 22 74 35
Daily 8 a.m.–3 a.m.
A smart, modern café-restaurant catering to a smart, modern crowd. Sophisticated Mediterranean food with hints of Asia and America. Large terrace. €

Dukatz
U-Bahn Odeonsplatz
Salvatorplatz 1
Tel. 2 91 96 00
Mon–Sat 10 a.m.–1 a.m.;
Sun 10 a.m.–7 p.m.
Restaurant Mon–Sat noon–2.30 and 6.30–11 p.m.
Attractive literary café with an upstairs art gallery. International and Italian dishes are served in the restaurant; small snacks in the café. Frequented by journalists, intellectuals and a trendy highbrow crowd. The lovely terrace is designed on the model of an Italian piazza. €€

El Gordo Loco
U-Bahn Lehel; S-Bahn Isartor
Tram 19 Max-Monument
Mariannenstr. 3
Tel. 21 26 83 55
Daily 5 p.m.–1 a.m.
A wide variety of dishes hailing from Mexico and Latin America. They prepare the juice gambas directly at your table.
Happy hour 5–8 p.m. €

Zum Franziskaner
U-Bahn Marienplatz or Odeonsplatz
S-Bahn Marienplatz
Tram 19 Theatinerstrasse or Nationaltheater
Perusastrasse 5
Tel. 231 81 20
Open 8 a.m.–midnight
The place to sample *Weisswurst*, Bavaria's most important contribution to Germany's sausage repertoire. It is made from ground veal and parsley and simmered in water—not boiled and certainly not fried. To follow Bavarian custom to the letter, be sure to eat your *Weisswurst* before noon and wash it down with a glass of *Weissbier*. €€

1. Münchner Kartoffelhaus
S-Bahn Marienplatz or Isartor
Hochbrückenstrasse 3
Tel. 29 63 31
Mon–Thurs noon–11 p.m.; Fri, Sat noon–midnight; Sun and holidays 5.30–11 p.m.
Cosy place to sample the potato in all its guises: soup, salad, snacks and main dishes with fish, meat or vegetarian. €

KÖNIGSPLATZ

Brasserie Tresznjewski
U-Bahn Königsplatz or Universität
Tram 27 Pinakotheken

- Theresienstrasse 72
- Tel. 28 23 49
- Sun–Wed 8 a.m.–1 a.m.;
- Thurs, Fri, Sat 8 a.m.–4 a.m.

A bright and breezy brasserie that is handy for lunch if you're at the Pinakotheks. Salads, sandwiches and wok dishes feature strongly, and it's big on breakfasts for early bird culture vultures. €

Cohen's
- U-Bahn Universität
- Tram 27 Pinakotheken
- Theresienstrasse 31
- Tel. 2 80 95 45
- Daily noon–midnight

Jewish (not kosher) and oriental cuisine in a genuine Art Deco ambiance. €

Deeba
- U-Bahn Theresienstrasse
- Tram 27 Pinakotheken
- Barer Strasse 42
- Tel. 28 34 07
- Sun–Fri 11.30 a.m.–3 p.m. and 5.30 p.m.–midnight,
- Sat 5.30 p.m.–midnight

Pakistani cuisine that gets frequent rave reviews in the local press. €

Meson Galicia
- U-Bahn Hohenzollernplatz or Josefsplatz
- Tram Hohenzollernplatz
- Augustenstrasse 62
- Tel. 54 21 23 55
- Daily 6 p.m.–1 a.m.

Hot and crispy *boquerones,* fresh salad, grilled fish—enough to make you dream of summer holidays in Spain. €

SCHWABING

Alter Simpl
- U-Bahn Universität
- Türkenstrasse 57
- Tel. 272 30 83
- Sun–Thurs 11 a.m.–3 a.m.;
- Fri, Sat 11 a.m.–4 a.m.

The haunt of Munich's leading writers and artists in the early 20th century, this café gave its name to *Simplicissimus,* a satirical magazine which proved to be a thorn in the side of the Bavarian establishment. Attractive dark-wood interior and decent daily menu. €

Café An Der Uni CADU
- U-Bahn Universität
- Ludwigstrasse 24
- Tel. 28 98 66 00
- Mon–Fri 8 a.m.–1 a.m.;
- Sat and Sun 9 a.m.–1 a.m.

This is a trendy hang-out for students at nearby Munich University, with tables put out on Ludwigstrasse in fine weather. Good for snacks, coffees and intellectually stimulating conversation. €

Dining Out

Café Reitschule
- U-Bahn Giselastrasse
- Königinstrasse 34
- Tel. 33 34 02
- Daily 9 a.m.–1 a.m.

The café terrace overlooks the neighbouring riding school. It's a chilled-out spot by day, but at night attracts a crowd that puts maximum effort into being "in". €–€€

Kaisergarten Schlank- und Speisemeisterei
- U-Bahn Münchener Freiheit
- Kaiserstrasse 34
- Tel. 34 02 02 03
- Daily 10 a.m.–1 a.m.

Wide range of modern Bavarian dishes with a Mediterranean influence. On weekdays, set lunches at very reasonable prices, even better when served beneath the chestnut trees. €–€€

Tantris
- U-Bahn Bonner Platz or Dietlindenstrasse
- Johann-Fichte-Strasse 7
- Tel. 3 61 95 90
- Tues–Sat noon–3 p.m. and 6.30 p.m.–1 a.m.

Widely accorded the title of Munich's number one restaurant. You'll find top-rank international cuisine here, plus an unlikely welcome from an odd collection of dragon statues outside the entrance. €€€

Wotrys
- U-Bahn Josephsplatz
- Neureuther Strasse 8
- Tel. 27 37 57 31
- Open daily 5 p.m.–1 a.m.

Greek tavern with a romantic, candle-lit atmosphere. Classic Greek cuisine with a French touch. Extensive wine list. €€–€€€

ENGLISCHER GARTEN

Restaurant am Chinesischen Turm
- U-Bahn Giselastrasse
- Bus 54, 154 Chinesischer Turm
- Tram 17 Tivolistrasse
- Englischer Garten 3
- Tel. 38 38 73 27
- Open daily 10 a.m.–midnight

This attractive *Gaststätte* offers reasonably priced daily specials and a more substantial alternative to the liquid sustenance consumed at the nearby beer garden. €

Seehaus
- U-Bahn Münchener Freiheit
- Kleinhesselohe 3
- Tel. 3 81 61 30
- Open daily 10 a.m.–1 a.m.

With its superb views over the Englischer Garten lake, this is one

Dining Out

of the most scenic lunchtime locations in the city. €€

HAIDHAUSEN

Le Bousquerey
S-Bahn Rosenheimer Platz
Rablstrasse 37
Tel. 48 84 55
Open daily 6 p.m.–1 a.m.
Effortless French style and excellent fish or meat specialities make this small, intimate restaurant an experience to be savoured. €€

Paros
U-Bahn Max-Weber-Platz
Kirchenstrasse 27
Tel. 4 70 29 95
Open daily 5 p.m.–1 a.m.
The relaxed, friendly atmosphere of the Greek islands recreated in this small corner of Munich. Roast lamb is the house speciality, but there are great fish dishes, too. €–€€

Preysing Garten
U-Bahn Max-Weber-Platz
S-Bahn Rosenheimer Platz
Preysingstrasse 69
Tel. 6 88 07 22
Daily 10 a.m.–1 a.m.
The century-old Preysing Garten has excellent and imaginative international cuisine, and a small beer garden for warm summer evenings. €

Vinaiolo
S-Bahn Rosenheimer Platz
Steinstrasse 42
Tel. 48 95 03 56
Tues–Sun noon–3 p.m. and 6.30 p.m.–1 a.m.;
Mon 6.30 p.m.–1 a.m.
Fine Italian cuisine, speedy service, comprehensive wine list. €€€

AROUND MUNICH

Maharadja
U-Bahn Maillingerstrasse
Blutenburgstrasse 79
Tel. 13 01 24 82
Open daily 11.30 a.m.–2 p.m. and 5.30 p.m.–midnight
Vast choice of Indian specialities, tasty lunch menus. €

Zum Koreaner
U-Bahn Maillingerstrasse
Nymphenburger Strasse 132
Tel. 18 98 59 93
Daily 11.30 a.m.–2.30 p.m. and 6 p.m.–midnight
Delicious Korean dishes. Organic meat, and no glutamate. €–€€

Zur Schwaige
U-Bahn Romanplatz
Schloss Nymphenburg 30
Tel. 17 44 21
Daily 10 a.m.–midnight
Lipsmacking Bavarian and international cuisine. €

Entertainment

Munich is one of Europe's most exciting entertainment capitals. The high point of the classical music year comes in the summer, with the Munich Philharmonic's *Münchner Klaviersommer* in June and July, and the July and August Summer Festival featuring opera and ballet. Information about what's on can be found in the English-language magazine *Munich Found*, or local listings papers such as *München im…*, *in München* and *Münchner Stadtmagazin*.

MAJOR ARTS VENUES

Deutsches Theater C 5
- U-Bahn Sendlinger Tor
- S-Bahn Karlsplatz
- Schwanthalerstrasse 13
- Tel. 55 23 44 44

Broadway-style shows and blockbuster musicals, as well as occasional operetta and ballet.

Gasteig F 6
- S-Bahn Rosenheimer Platz
- Tram 18 Am Gasteig
- Rosenheimer Strasse 5
- Tel. 54 81 81 81

The city's showcase for classical music has four main concert halls. The famous Munich Philharmonic plays at the Philharmonia Hall, while chamber works, smaller orchestral and World Music concerts can be heard in the Carl-Orff-Saal, Kleinen Konzertsaal and Black Box hall.

Münchner Kammerspiele E 5
- U-Bahn Marienplatz or Odeonsplatz
- S-Bahn Marienplatz
- Tram 19 Kammerspiele
- Maximilianstrasse 26–28
- Tel. 233 966 00 (bookings) or 54 81 81 81

Classic and modern drama by German playwrights and foreign authors translated into German is staged at this splendid Art Nouveau theatre, recently renovated.

Nationaltheater (Bayerische Staatsoper) E 5
- U-Bahn Marienplatz or Odeonsplatz
- S-Bahn Marienplatz
- Tram 19 Nationaltheater
- Max-Joseph-Platz 1
- Tel. 21 85 19 20

The Bavarian State Orchestra under Zubin Mehta provides the music—if you can't get in during the July

Entertainment

opera festival, check out the live big-screen transmissions on Max-Joseph-Platz. Also the seat of the Bavarian State Ballet.

Prinzregententheater H 5
- U-Bahn Prinzregentenplatz
- Prinzregentenplatz 12
- Tel. 21 85 28 99

Opera, ballet and concerts. Regular performances by the Bavarian Radio Symphony Orchestra.

Residenztheater (Bayerisches Staatsschauspiel) E 4
- U-Bahn Odeonsplatz
- S-Bahn Marienplatz
- Tram 19 Nationaltheater
- Max-Joseph-Platz 1
- Tel. 21 85 19 40
- Herkulessaal: tel. 2 90 67-263

There are two auditoriums in the Residenz's modern theatre: the Herkulessaal features orchestral works, the Max-Joseph-Saal presents chamber music.

Staatstheater am Gärtnerplatz D 6
- U-Bahn Fraunhoferstrasse
- Gärtnerplatz 3
- Tel. 21 85 19 60

This fine old theatre is predominantly used for operetta and the lighter end of the main operatic repertoire.

CHILDREN'S SHOWS

Circus Krone B 4
- S-Bahn Hackerbrücke
- Zirkus-Krone-Strasse 1–6, entrance on Marsstrasse
- Tel. 55 81 66

Famous old circus, sure to please the kids.

Marionettentheater D 6
- U-Bahn Sendlinger Tor
- Blumenstrasse 32
- Tel. 26 57 12 (10 a.m.–noon only)
- Closed Mon

Classic puppet fun for children, though more grown-up shows are also put on, with operas by Mozart and Carl Orff in the repertoire.

Münchner Theater für Kinder C 3
- U-Bahn Stiglmaierplatz
- Dauchauer Strasse 46
- Tel. 59 54 54/59 38 58

Lively performances of classical plays for children.

BEER HALLS AND GARDENS

The traditional Beer Halls and Beer Gardens are an essential part of Munich culture. Most of them are attached to a single brewery, and some —known as *Hausbrauereien*—produce their own beer to guarantee maximum freshness. They all serve food, mainly good standard Bavarian cuisine, and many have live bands to jolly things along. A word of warning: if a table has a sign saying Stammtisch don't sit there, as it's reserved for regular customers and you won't be served.

Augustinerkeller

- S-Bahn Hackerbrücke
- Tram 17 Hopfenstrasse
- Arnulfstrasse 52
- Tel. 59 43 93
- Daily 10 a.m.–midnight

A laid-back atmosphere, Augustiner beer and plenty of good foodstands make this 100-year-old beer hall and garden worth venturing beyond the Hauptbahnhof for.

Bavaria Bräu

- U-Bahn Theresienwiese
- Theresienhöhe 7
- Tel. 51 99 77 57
- Daily 9.30 a.m.–1 a.m.

You don't have to wait for the Oktoberfest to enjoy the pleasures of Theresienwiese. Overlooking the vast festival site is this much-loved beer hall (the former Pschorrkeller), with great beer and food year-round.

Chinesischer Turm

- U-Bahn Giselastrasse
- Bus 54, 154 Chinesischer Turm
- Tram 17 Tivolistrasse
- Englischer Garten 3
- Tel. 38 38 73 27
- Daily 10 a.m.–midnight

The 7,000 seats of this celebrated beer garden can easily be filled on a fine summer's afternoon. Some find it too touristy these days, but if you want the full Munich experience a visit is virtually obligatory.

Hirschgarten

- S-Bahn Laim
- Hirschgarten 1
- Tel. 17 25 91
- Daily 9 a.m.–midnight

Located next to a deer park not far from Schloss Nymphenburg, this is one of the city's most pleasant places to quaff a litre or two of Bavaria's finest. There are shooting galleries and merry-go-rounds, too.

Hofbräuhaus

- U-Bahn, S-Bahn Marienplatz
- Platzl 9
- Tel. 22 16 76
- Daily 9 a.m.–midnight

Without doubt the most famous beer hall in Munich—and not just because it's where Hitler's political career began. It's big, noisy, and will give you a genuine sense of what beer-hall culture is all about. There are also nightly oompah bands and a pleasant garden out the back.

Entertainment

Hofbräukeller
- U-Bahn Max-Weber-Platz
- Tram 18 Wiener Platz
- Tram 19 Maximilaneum
- Innere Wiener Strasse 19
- Tel. 4 59 92 50
- Daily 9 a.m.–midnight.
- Beer garden 11 a.m.–10.30 p.m.

This huge, rambling beer hall in the heart of Haidhausen has character by the barrel-load, as well as a Jazzkeller and Maratanga "dance café" in the basement. Small playground, and Kinderland, an area for children, in the restaurant.

Löwenbräukeller
- U-Bahn Stiglmaierplatz
- Nymphenburger Strasse 2
- Tel. 52 60 21
- Daily 10 a.m.–10.30 a.m.

Oozing the earthy charm of a genuine old Munich beer hall, the Löwenbräukeller shouldn't be missed. Situated next to the Löwenbräu brewery, it serves up excellent beer and food and has a fine beer garden as well.

Paulaner am Nockherberg
- U-Bahn Kolumbusplatz or Silberhornstrasse
- Tram 25, 27 Ostfriedhof
- Hochstrasse 77
- Tel. 45 99 13-0
- Daily 10 a.m.–1 a.m.;
- Beer garden 11 a.m.–midnight

An impressive building in turn-of-the-century style. The traditional opening of the strong beer season takes place with much pomp and circumstance. Fine Bavarian cuisine, mingling traditional and modern tastes. Huge array of Paulaner beers.

Paulaner Bräuhaus
- U-Bahn Goetheplatz
- Kapuzinerplatz 5
- Tel. 5 44 61 10
- Daily 10 a.m.–1 a.m.

A gigantic *Hausbrauerei* complete with copper brewing apparatus behind the bar. The *Weissbier* is one of the best in Munich.

BARS AND JAZZ CLUBS
Munich's long-standing reputation as a jazz-loving city is borne out at the numerous clubs and regular city-wide festivals.

Atzinger
- U-Bahn Universität
- Schellingstrasse 9
- Tel. 28 28 80
- Mon–Sat 10 a.m.–3 a.m.,
- Sun 10 a.m.–1 a.m.

Popular meeting place for students and artists near the University.

Café am Beethovenplatz (Mariandl)
- U-Bahn Goetheplatz
- Goethestrasse 51

- Tel. 54 40 43 48
- Daily 9 a.m.–1 a.m.

Food and all kinds of music in a classy atmosphere.

Dreigroschenkeller
- U-Bahn Fraunhoferstrasse
- S-Bahn Rosenheimer Platz
- Tram 18 Deutsches Museum
- Lilienstrasse 2
- Tel. 4 89 02 90
- Daily 5 p.m.–1 a.m.

Fun, alternative theme pub based on Brecht's Threepenny Opera. The food and drink are good, too.

Hard Rock Café
- U-Bahn, S-Bahn Marienplatz
- Platz 1
- Tel. 2 42 94 00
- Sun–Thurs noon–1 a.m.; Fri and Sat noon–2 a.m.

Live music and all-American specialities from Caesar Salad to hamburgers, opposite the Hofbräuhaus.

Jazzclub Unterfahrt
- U-Bahn Max-Weber-Platz
- Tram 18, 19
- Einsteinstrasse 44
- Tel. 4 48 27 94
- Daily 7.30 p.m.–1 a.m.

One of Munich's premier jazz venues, with top German and international jazz outfits through the week and great Sunday-night jam sessions. You can whet your appetite with a pre-gig drink at the adjacent Unionsbräu beer hall.

Max-Emanuel-Brauerei
- U-Bahn Universität
- Tram N27 Scellingstrasse
- Adalbertstrasse 33
- Tel. 2 71 51 58
- Sun–Fri 11 a.m.–1 a.m., Sat 11 a.m.–3 a.m.

A genuine eccentric—part beer garden, part student bar, part restaurant, and with a dance club offering salsa and tango nights.

Muffathalle
- S-Bahn Rosenheimer Platz or Isartor
- Tram 18 Deutsches Museum
- Zellstrasse 4
- Tel. 45 87 50 10 (information) or 45 87 50 00

Delightful "alternative" venue with excellent café and a romantic beer garden in summer.

Night Club im Bayerischen Hof
- U-Bahn, S-Bahn Karlsplatz
- Tram 19 Maffeistrasse
- Promenadenplatz 2–6
- Tel. 212 09 94
- Daily 8 p.m.–3 a.m.

Chic club drawing the great names of international jazz, as well as reggae, funk and blues musicians.

Entertainment

Podium
- U-Bahn Münchener Freiheit
- Wagnerstrasse 1
- Tel. 39 94 82
- Sun–Thurs 8 p.m./1 a.m.,
- Fri, Sat 8 p.m.–3 a.m.

A well-known Schwabing club that swings to Dixieland jazz on Mondays, and rock and "oldie" bands on other nights.

CLUBLAND

For a culture shock, spend your evening in a beer hall listening to a rollicking brass band, then sound out the scene in some of the trendiest discos and nightclubs in Germany.

Atomic Café
- U-Bahn, S-Bahn Marienplatz or Isartor
- Neuturmstrasse 5
- Tel. 30 77 72 32
- From 9 p.m. on concert nights, otherwise from 10 p.m.

Centrally located dance club with a penchant for 1970s retro.

Kultfabrik
- U-Bahn, S-Bahn Ostbahnhof
- Gratinger Strasse 6
- Information. tel. 49 00 90 70

An amazing disco metropolis in Haidhausen that outdoes anything you'll find in New York, London or Berlin. A staggering variety of nightclubs and discos (and places to snack when you need an energy boost) on one site, running the gamut of dance music, from garage to grunge, from psychedelic to soul.

Nachtwerk
- S-Bahn Donnersbergerbrücke
- Tram 18, 19 Alter Lokschuppen
- Landsberger Strasse 185
- Tel. 59 98 96 40
- Fri, Sat 10 p.m.–4 a.m.

Reasonably priced club west of the city centre, where you're likely to hear dance chart music.

Optimolwerke
- U-Bahn, S-Bahn Ostbahnhof
- Friedenstrasse 10
- Tel. 450 69 20

No less than 13 discos and clubs.

Parkcafé
- U-Bahn, S-Bahn Karlsplatz
- Sophienstrasse 7
- Tel. 59 83 13
- Wed–Sat 9 p.m.–4 a.m.

Extremely popular disco in an elegant Jugendstil building at the Alter Botanischer Garten.

4004
- U-Bahn Westendstrasse
- Tram 18, 19 Alter Lokschuppen
- Landsberger Strasse 169–175
- Sat and eves of holidays
- 10 p.m.–5 a.m.

Four clubs, 12 bars on one ticket.

The Hard Facts

Airport
Munich's ultra-modern Franz-Josef-Strauss Flughafen is 28 km (17 miles) northeast of the city. For general airport information, dial the central switchboard on 975 00. For flight information, dial 97 52 13 13.

S-Bahn suburban trains run to the city centre every 20 minutes from 4 a.m. to 1 a.m., with a journey time of 40 minutes. (Sat and Sun from 5.31 a.m.) Lines S1 and S8 both stop at the Hauptbahnhof (main railway station) and Marienplatz. To get to the centre of Munich you will need to buy a ticket that covers four zones (see Transport).

Other options include the Lufthansa airport bus, available for all airline passengers, which costs 9.50€ (15€ return), single ticket for children 4,50€. It takes 45 minutes to get to Arnulfstrasse near the Hauptbahnhof (tel. 01 805 838 426 or www.autobus.oberbayern.de for reservations).

Taxis are expensive. A ride to the centre will set you back around 60€.

Bicycle Hire
With 1,300 km of cycle paths, Munich is ideal for visiting on wheels. You can hire a bike at Radius-Touristik, tel. 59 61 13, in the main railway station, platform 32, open daily May–Sept 10 a.m.–6 p.m., April and Oct on fine days only. Guided bicycle tours are arranged for groups.

Climate
With the Alps virtually at its doorstep, Munich's weather can be extremely changeable and there's the chance of rain—or sunshine for that matter—at any time of year. Having said that, summers are usually warm, with the daytime average in July reaching 23°C (73°F), while spring and autumn can be delightfully mild, fresh and sunny. Winter temperatures can plummet, with the thermometer rarely rising above freezing in January and February and frequent snowfall.

Communications
Post offices are normally open Mon–Fri 9 a.m.–6 p.m. and Sat 9 a.m.–noon. The main post office, opposite the Hauptbahnhof on Bahnhofplatz 1, keeps longer hours, opening Mon–Fri 7.30 a.m.–8 p.m., Sat 9 a.m.–4 p.m. Fax, telephone and currency exchange facilities are available here, as well as stamp vending machines. Stamps can also be bought at some tobacconists and souvenir shops.

The Hard Facts

Telephone. To make international calls from Munich, dial 00 + country code + number. The international code for Germany is 49, the area code for Munich is 089. You can make overseas calls from public pay phones (which are always cheaper than using the phone in your hotel room). Most of them now only take phonecards, available from post offices, tourist offices, T-Punkt branches of the German Telekom and some newsstands at 5€ and 10€. Off-peak rates start on weekdays at 6 p.m., become even cheaper at 9 p.m. and last until 8 a.m. They also apply at weekends. Note that not all phone boxes can operate reverse-charge calls; those that do have a ringing symbol on them.

The Munich Internet Service Center is at Im Tal 31, between Marienplatz and Isartor, and opens 24 hours a day.

Useful numbers:
Domestic Directory Enquiries
11833
International Directory Enquiries
11834
International operator
0180 200 10 33

Customs
European Union (EU) regulations apply. For those travelling to Germany from other countries within the EU there is no limit on the import of duty-paid goods for personal consumption. For EU residents there is still an official duty-free import allowance of 200 cigarettes, one litre of spirits and 5 litres of wine. Non-EU residents are usually restricted to the same quantities other than the amount of wine, which in most cases is 2 litres.

Disabled
Most of the major museums, theatres, cinemas, train stations, public buildings and the S-Bahn (commuter) trains, trams and buses have been either specifically designed or else modified to make them accessible to visitors in wheelchairs. The U-Bahn carriages still present problems, however, as sometimes the entrances make them difficult to board.

Club Behinderter und ihrer Freunde e.V. München (CBF), Joh.-Fichte-Str. 12, can arrange for trained assistants to accompany disabled travellers around the city and to concerts and the opera. Call 356 88 08, Mon, Wed, Fri 9 a.m.–1 p.m.; Tues, Thurs 9 a.m.–4 p.m.

Driving
Congested roads, confusing one-way routes and a lack of free parking, combined with a superb public transport system, mean there's not much incen-

tive to bring a car into Munich. If you decide to brave it, look out for car parks *(Parkhäuser)* such as the Tiefgarage vor der Oper on Max-Joseph-Platz (580 spaces), open 24 hours a day; or Am Stachus (385 spaces), open Mon–Wed 7 a.m.–midnight; Thurs–Sat 7 a.m.–2 a.m., Sun and holidays 10 a.m.–midnight; Motorent at Gasteig (300 spaces), open round the clock; Am Färbegraben (550 spaces), weekdays 7 a.m.–midnight.

You can use Park & Ride, leaving your car free of charge at a car park outside town and taking a U-Bahn or S-Bahn into the centre. Park & Ride Fröttmaning (1,270 spaces), BAB 9 Exit Fröttmaning, open round the clock, 17-minute link by U-Bahn 6 to Marienplatz.

Note that trams always have right of way and should never be overtaken when they are at passenger stops.

A car is very useful if you plan to do a lot of touring beyond Munich. Outside the city you will find an encircling *Autobahn* (motorway), which gives access to all directions in Germany. The recommended upper speed limit on the Autobahn is 130 kph (80 mph). The limit in town is 50 kph (30 mph) and 80–100 kph (50–62 mph) on country roads.

Service stations can be found every 40 km (25 miles) or so on the motorways. Most are self-service and take credit cards. Unleaded fuel is *bleifrei*, diesel is *Benzin* or *Diesel*, oil is *Öl*.

If you bring your own car, be sure to carry your driving licence, car registration document, valid insurance certificate (check that your insurance covers driving in Germany before you leave), first-aid kit and red warning triangle, which must be placed behind the vehicle if you break down on the *Autobahn*.

The main automobile club in Germany is ADAC *(Allgemeiner Deutscher Automobilclub)*, tel. 01805 10 11 12. For the ADAC emergency road service, dial 01802 22 22 22. It's worth finding out from your own automobile club before you leave whether it is affiliated to one in Germany, and if so what services you are entitled to use.

A simpler option might be to hire a car. All the big car-hire firms have offices at the airport and the Hauptbahnhof. You might also try local firms, which often have good deals on offer. You will need to show a valid driving licence, be over 21 (in most cases), and have a credit card for the deposit.

Avis:
Hauptbahnhof, tel. 550 22 51
Bookings: 0180 5 55 77 55

Europcar:
Hauptbahnhof, tel. 550 13 41
Bookings: 018 5 80 00

Hertz:
  Hauptbahnhof, tel. 550 22 56
  Bookings: 0180 5 33 35 35

Sixt Budget:
  Hauptbahnhof, tel. 550 24 47;
  Bookings: 0180 5 25 25 25

Emergencies

The emergency telephone number for the police is 110; for an ambulance 19 222 (prefix 089 for cell phones); fire brigade 112. For urgent medical attention, call 01805 19 12 12.

The Pharmacy Emergency Service is on 59 44 75. A designated international (i.e. English-speaking) pharmacy is the Ludwigs-Apotheke München, Neuhauser Strasse 11, tel. 18 94 03 00, open Mon–Sat 9 a.m.–8 p.m.

If you require dental treatment, call the *Zahnärztlicher Notdienst* (Dental Emergency Service) on 7 23 30 93.

Drogenberatung deals with drug-related problems; tel. 23 32 28 44 (Mon–Thurs 9 a.m.–5 p.m., Fri 9 a.m.–3 p.m.). Helpline (Sucht-Hotline) 28 28 22.

There's a casualty department at Munich's large central hospital, the Klinikum Innenstadt der Ludwig-Maximilian-Universität, Ziemssenstrasse 1 (internal medicine) or the surgical clinic, Chirurgische Klinik, Nussbaumstrasse 20, tel. 516 00.

EU nationals are entitled to free medical care, but should hold a European health insurance card.

Formalities

In the case of EU citizens, visitors will only require a valid passport or National Identity Card to enter Germany. Nationals of the United States, Canada, Australia and New Zealand can stay for up to 90 days on a valid passport without needing a visa.

Language

Even fluent German-speakers may find themselves caught out in Munich, where up to 30 per cent of the population use a version of the Bavarian dialect. Everyone speaks standard German as well. Staff at most large hotels, shops and restaurants speak English, and it is also widely understood among the general population, especially by younger people. Initiating a conversation in German always goes down well, though, and it can be fun to try out even a few basic phrases.

Good morning	*Guten Morgen*
Good day	*Grüss Gott*
Good evening	*Guten Abend*
Goodbye	*Auf Wiedersehen*
Yes/No	*Ja/Nein*
Please	*Bitte*
Thank you	*Danke*
Where is…?	*Wo ist…?*
left/right	*links/rechts*
straight ahead	*gerade aus*

I need…	*Ich brauche…*
How much is that?	*Wieviel macht es?*
cheap	*billig*
expensive	*teuer*
I'd like…	*Ich hätte gern…*
The bill, please	*Zahlen, bitte*

Lost and Found

If you lose something on a tram, a city bus or around town, contact the *Fundbüro der Landeshauptstadt München* (Lost Property Office), Ötztaler Strasse 17, Mon–Thurs 8 a.m.–noon, Fri 7 a.m.–noon, Tues also 2 p.m.–6.30 p.m.; tel. 233 00.

For items lost on the U-Bahn, go to the MVG Infopoint at the main railway station, Mon–Fri 8 a.m.–noon and 12.30–4 p.m., Sat and Sun 9 a.m.–12.30 and 1–5 p.m.; tel. 21 91 32 40. Finds are kept here for one day then sent to the Lost Property Office (address above). For the S-Bahn or trains, try the *Fundstelle im Hauptbahnhof* in the main hall, open Mon–Fri 6.30 a.m.–11.30 p.m., Sat 7.30 a.m.–10.45 p.m., Sun and holidays 7.30 a.m.–11 p.m., tel. 13 08 66 64.

If property has been lost at the airport, call 97 52 13 70.

Money Matters

Banks generally open Mon–Fri 8.30 a.m.–12.30 p.m. and 1.30 p.m.–4 p.m., Thurs until 6 p.m. (some stay open at lunch time) and some close at 3 p.m. on Friday. Bank offices at the airport and main railway station keep longer hours and are also open at weekends. Exchange bureaux *(Wechselstuben)* for cash and traveller's cheques can be found around town, and money can also be changed at the central post office and savings banks *(Sparkasse)*.

Currency. The euro, divided into 100 cents.

Cash cards. You can draw cash with your ordinary cash card, if it carries the Eurocheque, Visa or MasterCard symbol, at most ATM machines using your regular PIN code number.

Credit cards can be used in larger hotels, restaurants and shops, though this is still very much a cash-based society.

Travellers cheques are widely accepted throughout Munich—don't forget that you need your passport to cash them.

Public Holidays

Be prepared to find Munich's banks, shops and many of its restaurants, galleries and museums closed on the following public holidays:

January 1	New Year's Day
January 6	Epiphany
May 1	Labour Day
August 15	Assumption
October 3	Day of National Unity

The Hard Facts

November 1 — All Saints' Day
December 25 — Christmas Day
December 26 — Boxing Day

Moveable:
March/April — Good Friday
Easter Monday
May — Ascension Day
May/June — Whit Monday
June — Corpus Christi
3rd Wed in November — Day of Prayer and Repentance

Safety
Munich is by and large a safe city for travellers, though it's always sensible to take a few basic precautions. Only carry the money you will need for the day along with a credit card and ATM card. Be careful with valuables, wallets, cameras, etc., as there is always the risk of pickpocketing in crowded places such as the Hauptbahnhof.

In theory, the police can ask you for proof of identity at any time, so it's a good idea to carry your passport just in case.

Tipping
A service charge will automatically be added to all hotel and restaurant bills, though it is still customary to leave a small tip by rounding off the amount. The same applies to taxi drivers, while hotel porters are usually given 50 cents per bag, lavatory attendants 25 cents and hotel maids about 5€ per week.

Toilets
Public conveniences are found in plentiful supply around Munich in museums, cafés and restaurants, hotels, department stores and railway stations. Some have attendants, who should be given a small gratuity. They are signposted as W.C., and marked *Herren* (for men) *Damen* (for women), or simply have male and female figures.

Tourist Information
For free maps, brochures and information on what's on, call at the Fremdenverkehrsamt:

Fremdenverkehrsamt München
Sendlinger Str. 1,
80313 Munich
Tel. 233-9 65 00
Call Center: Mon–Fri 8 a.m.–7 p.m., Sat 9 a.m.–5 p.m.
www.muenchen-tourist.de

Main railway station
Bahnhofsplatz 2
Mon–Sat 9 a.m.–8 p.m. (Nov–Mar 9.30 a.m.–6.30 p.m.); Sun (year round) 10 a.m.–6 p.m.

Neues Rathaus (town hall)
Marienplatz
Mon–Fri 10 a.m.–8 p.m.,
Sat 10 a.m.–4 p.m.

Bavarian region: *Tourismusverband München-Oberbayern*
Bodenseestrasse 113
tel. 8 29 21 80
Mon–Thurs 9 a.m.–noon and 1–4 p.m., Fri 9 a.m.–12.30 p.m.

The Hard Facts

Transport

Munich's first-rate public transport network of trams, buses, U-Bahn (underground) and S-Bahn (suburban) trains is operated by the Münchner Verkehrs-Verbund (MVV), tel. 41 42 43 44 or 21 03 30 for information). The system operates weekdays from about 5 a.m. to 0.30 a.m., weekends till 1.30 a.m., with night buses after this time.

Tickets can be purchased at the blue MVV vending machines found at U- and S-Bahn stations, on buses, at tram stops and at newsagents and tobacconists that have a white "K" on display. The same ticket is valid across the network for up to 2 hours in the same direction.

A single ticket (*Kurzstreckenkarte*) costs 1.10€ for journeys of four stops or less, 2.20€ across one zone, 4.40€ across two zones, 6.60€ across three, 8.80€ for four or more. Better value is the *Streifenkarte*, or strip-card. For a journey anywhere within one zone you need to cancel two strips (one strip for children): a strip-card of ten costing 10.50€ therefore gives you five rides within a zone. For a ride to the airport, four zones from the centre, you cancel eight strips. Always validate your ticket at the blue cancelling machine near the platform before getting onto a train; for buses and trams, the machine is inside the vehicle. Plain-clothed inspectors make regular spot checks, and those without a ticket face on-the-spot fines of 40€.

If you're doing a lot of travelling around the city, the best option is a day ticket (*Tageskarte*): 4.80€ for the inner zone (*Innenraum*), 6.50€ for the outer zone (*München XXL*), and 9.60€ to cover them all (*Gesamtnetz*). A three-day inner zone pass is 11.80€. With a "Partner" card, up to five people can travel together; 8.50€ for one day on the inner zone, 11.50€ on XXL and 17€ on the whole network. A 3-day Partner card for the inner zone costs 20€.

DB (Deutsche Bahn) trains. You can reach all areas of the region, as well as cities in Germany and throughout Europe, using the efficient German railways. For information or reservations call 11 8 61.

Taxis. Munich's beige taxis are something of a luxury in a city so well served by its public transport. Taxi ranks are located near most tourist sites and the main railway stations. To book in advance, call Taxi München e.G. on 21 610 and 1 94 10.

Voltage

Electric current is 220-volt 50-cycle AC, and sockets are for plugs with two round pins. British and American equipment will require an adaptor.

Index

Ainmillerstrasse 35
Akademie der
  bildenden Künste
  34–35
Alte Akademie 21
– Pinakothek 31
Alter Botanischer
  Garten 22
Alter Hof 15–16
Altes Rathaus 15
Amalienburg 43
Ammersee 48–49
Andechs 49
Antikensammlungen
  28
Archäologische
  Staatssammlung 38
Arts venues 58–59
Asamkirche 19
Badenburg 43
Bavaria Filmstadt
  44–45
Bayerische
  Staatsbibliothek 33
– Staatskanzlei 26
Bayerisches
  Nationalmuseum
  37–38
Beer halls 59–61
Bier und Oktober-
  festmuseum 17
BMW Museum
  Zeithorizont 43–44
Bürgersaal 21
Chiemsee 49
Chinesischer Turm
  36, 60

Circus Krone 59
Clubs 63
Cuvilliés-Theater 25
Dachau 44
Deutsches Jagd- und
  Fischereimuseum
  20
– Museum 40
– Theater 58
Discos 63
Dom 20
Dreifaltigkeitskirche
  22
Englischer Garten 36
Erzbischöfliches-
  Palais 22
Feldherrnhalle 27
Fischbrunnen 14–15
forum am deutschen
  museum 40
Fraueninsel 49
Frauenkirche 20
Friedensengel 39
Gasteig 58
Glyptothek 28–29
Haidhausen 39–40
Haus der Kunst 38
Heiliggeistkirche
  17–18
Hellabrunn Zoo 44
Herrsching 48–49
Hochschule für
  Musik 30
Hofbräuhaus 16, 60
Hofgarten 26
Hohenschwangau
  46–48

Hohenzollernstrasse
  35
Jazz clubs 61–62
Johanniskirche 40
Jüdisches Museum
  München 19
Justizpalast 22
Karlsplatz 22
Karolinenplatz
  30–31
Kaufingerstrasse 19
Kleinhesseloher See
  36
Königsplatz 28–29
Kunsthalle der
  Hypo-
  Kulturstiftung 27
Kultfabrik 63
Gedenkstätte
  Dachau 44
Lenbachhaus 29–30
– Kunstbau 30
Leopoldstrasse
  34–35
Linderhof 48
Ludwig-
  Maximilians-
  Universität 34
Ludwigskirche
  33–34
Ludwigstrasse 33
Marienplatz 14
Mariensäule 14
Marionettentheater
  59
Marstallmuseum 41
Maximilianstrasse 27

Index

Maximilianeum 27
Maximilianpark 39
Max-Joseph-Platz 23
Michaelskirche 21
Monopteros 36
Müller'sches Volksbad 40
Münchner Kammerspiele 58
– Stadtmuseum 18–19
– Theater für Kinder 59
Nationaltheater 23, 58–59
Neue Pinakothek 31–32
Neues Rathaus 15
Neuhauser Strasse 19
Neuschwanstein 46
Oberammergau 48
Oktoberfest 45
Olympia Park 43
Palais Montgelas 22
– Portia 22
– Törring 23
Paläontologisches Museum 30
Peterskirche 18–19
Pinakothek der Moderne 32
Porcelain Museum 41
Prinzregententheater 59
Promenadeplatz 22

Propyläen 28
Residenzmuseum 23–25
Residenztheater 59
Schack-Galerie 38
Schatzkammer der Residenz 25
Schloss Berg 49
– Herrenchiemsee 49
– Nymphenburg 41
Siegestor 34
Spielzeugmuseum 15
Staatliches Museum Ägyptischer Kunst 25
– für Völkerkunde 27
Staatstheater am Gärtnerplatz 59
Starnberger See 49
Theatermuseum 26
Theatinerhof 27
Theatinerkirche 26
Theatron 43
Theresienwiese 44, 45
Valentin-Karlstadt-Musäum 16–17
Viktualienmarkt 18
Villa Stuck 39
Wedekindplatz 35
Welcome Card 32
Wiener Platz 39–40
Wittelsbacher Brunnen 22

GENERAL EDITOR
Barbara Ender-Jones
EDITOR
Christina Grisewood
LAYOUT
Luc Malherbe
PHOTO CREDITS
Huber/R. Schmid pp. 1, 5 17, 29, 37, 52;
Huber/Gräfenheim: p. 2;
Huber/Alfeld: pp. 6, 24, 42;
Huber/Reiter: p. 35;
Huber/Giovanni: p. 47;
Huber/Stauffenberg inside front cover
MAPS
Kartographie Huber

Copyright © 2006, 2000 by JPM Publications S.A. 12, avenue William-Fraisse, 1006 Lausanne, Switzerland
E-mail: information@jpmguides.com
Web site: http://www.jpmguides.com/

All rights reserved. No part of this book may be reproduced or transmitted in any form or by any means, electronic or mechanical, including photocopying, recording or by any information storage and retrieval system without permission in writing from the publisher.
Every care has been taken to verify the information in the guide, but neither the publisher nor his client can accept responsibility for any errors that may have occurred. If you spot an inaccuracy or a serious omission, please let us know.

Printed in Switzerland
Weber/Bienne (CTP) — 06/05/01
Edition 2006–2007